1ST 1990

D1809017

Under Steam and Sail
Reminiscences of a Sea Captain

Under Steam & Sail

Reminiscences of a Sea Captain

CAPTAIN
J A
WILSON

The Book Guild Ltd
Sussex, England

This book is sold subject to the condition that it shall not, by way of trade or otherwise, be lent, re-sold, hired out, photocopied or held in any retrieval system, or otherwise circulated without the publisher's prior consent or otherwise circulated in any form of binding or cover other than that in which this is published and without a similar condition including this condition being imposed on the subsequent purchaser.

———

The Book Guild Ltd.
25 High Street,
Lewes, Sussex.

First published 1990
© Captain John A. Wilson 1990
Set in Baskerville
Typesetting by Litho Link Ltd.,
Welshpool, Powys.
Printed in Great Britain by
Antony Rowe Ltd.,
Chippenham, Wiltshire.

British Library Cataloguing in Publication Data
Wilson, John (John Aage), *1916–*
    Under steam and sail: Reminiscences of a sea captain
    1. Merchant shipping. Biographies
    I. Title
    387.5′092′4

ISBN 0 86332 458 4

CONTENTS

PROLOGUE

Alexandre Dumas Junior expressed the opinion that 'an autobiography must be devoid of meaning because of the fact that no one ventures to confide to paper the crucial incidents in one's life'.

Plutarch says that 'every human being has at least one "skeleton" which he will die rather than unveil'.

Voltaire says that 'in any confession there is a crime which is never admitted'.

What was it that made me different? But how could it be otherwise? Wholly and solely pluck and the flow of high spirits — a sense of bluff which perhaps forms the first acts of men, if they ever commence. Bluff: that makes a man stretch his powers again and again, until he reaches his true self.

INTRODUCTION

Sea Captain John Aage Wilson was born in Arendal, Norway, in 1916, the son of Sea Captain John Wilson, a Norwegian shipowner, and the descendant of several generations of sea captains and shipowners.

Upon completion of his education in Norway, he joined the Norwegian Mercantile Marine in order to gain a thorough knowledge of the operation of ships. After sufficient practical experience to qualify for entering the Norwegian Merchant Marine Academy, he returned to Norway, and after two and a half years graduated with excellent marks.

Subsequent experience in various capacities at officer rank entitled him to the licence of Ship Master. He then worked with his father on their shipping business until the decease of the latter in 1940, whereupon he obtained his commercial letter and resumed management, registering his company in Oslo.

In order to increase the freedom of scope available to him, Sea Captain Wilson decided to transfer his one remaining ship to Panamanian registry, having in the meantime become a resident and citizen of Panama.

In April 1952 Sea Captain Wilson registered his company, Oceanwide Steamship Company, Inc., in Liberia, and in December of the same year he invested some of the cash surplus in American and Overseas Chartering Corporation, Inc., and American corporation.

In 1954 Sea Captain Wilson began negotiations for the construction of additional bulk carriers and concluded long term charters with the Chilean Nitrate Sales Corporation, New York and Santiago. He formed a new company, Ocean

Transport Lines, Inc., in Liberia, making the Oceanwide Steamship Co., Inc., into a holding company.

Together with his brother, Sea Captain Sigfried Wilson, they started up the Wilson Shipping Company in Santiago, Chile, from where the companies then operated.

In 1971 the office in Santiago was closed, and Sea Captain Sigfried Wilson established himself in Skagen, Denmark. The remaining two ships were sold in 1972.

Sea Captain Wilson has a far wider practical knowledge than most ship masters. He has continued his studies of technical advancements in the ship construction field and has himself designed many new and advanced features which have been incorporated in the company's ships, proving to be extremely practical in operation. His personal supervision of the construction of the ships proved to be of great value, and his experience and intimate knowledge of ship operation has enabled him to operate with unusual efficiency and economy.

Sea Captain Wilson speaks English, German, Spanish and Norwegian.

Sea Captain Wilson is president of the Holding Company Oceanwide Steamship Company, Inc., and Vice-President of Ocean Transport Lines, Inc. He is married and has four children. His residence is Panama, Republic of Panama.

During the years 1966-1970, Sea Captain Wilson was officer of the Company's sail-training ship, the Barquentine *Regina Maris* , and after a voyage of exploration to Cape Horn, Drake's Passage and the southern extremes of South America was elected member of *The Explorers' Club*, New York. On his return to Norway he received his licence as Master of Sailing Ships.

After his passage round Cape Horn he was elected member of the highest rank in the fashionable club, the *Association Amicale Internationale des Capitaines au Long Cours CAP-HORNIERS*, with the special distinction of having been the youngest member to have made this trip in command of a sailing cargo vessel.

He also received the *Medaille des Marins de Saint-Malo* upon his arrival in Saint-Malo from Cape Horn, awarded by the Mayor of the city during a formal reception at the Town Hall. In Australia he was elected Member of Honour of *The Australian Cape Horn Club*, now amalgamated with the aforementioned original Club of Saint-Malo.

Upon arrival in Oslo after the voyage he was granted an audience with His Majesty King Olav V in the Royal Palace, and His Majesty subsequently paid a visit to the ship.

During the Cape Horn Congress in Oslo in 1968 he was awarded the exclusive *Cape Horn Medal*.

The Norwegian King, Olav V, His Royal Highness Prince Philip, Duke of Edinburgh, His Majesty the King of Sweden, His Royal Highness the Prince of Denmark and the present President of France are all Members of Honour and Protectors of the Club.

In New York Sea Captain Wilson was knighted by His Majesty King Peter II of Yugoslavia to the *Order of St John of Jerusalem*. He has now been raised to the rank of Knight Commander Grand Cross of Justice.

Sea Captain Wilson was also decorated for active service during the German invasion of Norway, for partaking in the Underground Resistance, and for his eighteen months' imprisonment with hard labour during the Occupation. He was also decorated with the *Royal Yugoslav Commemorative War Cross — 1941-45*.

Sea Captain Wilson is a member of the Royal Norwegian Yachting Association and Member of Honour of the Royal Sydney Yacht Squadron. He is a member of Club Union, SA, Panama.

From 1969-70 Sea Captain Wilson circumnavigated the world from Norway via the Cape of Good Hope to Australia with the *Regina Maris* to represent Norway during the Bicentenary celebration of Captain James Cook's discovery of that continent. On his return he was awarded *The Medal of St Olav* for his accomplishment and for his contribution to relations between Norway and Australia.

During this voyage he also carried dispatches from the First Sea Lord, Admiral Sir Michael Le Fanu, GCB, of the British Admiralty, to the Chief of Australian Naval Staff, Vice-Admiral Sir Victor Smith, KBE, CB, DSC, and to the Prime Minister of Australia, J.G. Norton, Esq. The former received these despatches on board the *Regina Maris* in Sydney and simultaneously entrusted similar dispatches for the British Admiralty, which were delivered at the Admiralty in London to the then First Sea Lord, Admiral Sir Peter Hill-Norton,

KCB.

Sea Captain Wilson was commended in a letter from the authorities of Talcahuano, Chile, for his bravery in risking his life in a successful attempt to save the lives of four workers trapped by fire, a task made the more difficult and dangerous by the gas given off by burning nitrate of soda.

During his ship's call at Funchal in Madeira, Sea Captain Wilson, finding the tree planted by Captain James Cook two hundred years before now dead, took the initiative of planting a new one. This event aroused such interest that the planting was attended by the highest military and civil authorities, and was blessed by the Archbishop. A bronze plaque was donated by the ship's crew to commemorate the event, and stands in a prominent place near the site of the original tree.

In June 1972 Sea Captain Wilson was designated *Chargé d'affaires* for his adopted country, the Republic of Panama, in Norway.

1

From My Memorandum Book

The age of piracy is not dead. It will only be so when there is nothing left for the taking.

What you were expecting when you acquired this confession I cannot say, but I can give you an idea of what you will not get. If you wanted a tale of love, or a swashbuckling adventure on the high seas, or a hair-raising creepy with bony fingers scratching at your window in the small hours of a stormy night, then my advice to you is simple: put the book down and go fill your glass . . . . What you are going to get is *Truth*. Perhaps an unusual word for you, I know, and few of us have very much to do with it. But, since I am by no means a writer, I am not in the business of fabrication and therefore this book deals only with reality, sometimes harsh but always *true*. The Americans in their eternally adolescent Cagney-style would call it 'the low-down' — how it is done. How, for example, a man who has been at rock bottom more than once can somehow claw his way up again.

There is another unusual word for you: 'smuggling: this time you, like most honest people, *have* had something to do with it — although only in a small way, of course. Somewhere in *Twelfth Night* Shakespeare uses the expression 'Sport royal, I warrant you!' to which I would add: 'And before God, absolutely no sin'. We could define smuggling as taking into a country a commodity at a price forbidden by the bureaucracy of the day to the underdogs. The 'sport' may not be as old as prostitution and undoubtedly has fewer customers. Still, it is far less immoral, even though it carries much heavier penalties. I do not refer here to evil contraband such as narcotics and weapons — I mean the simple everyday luxuries the underdogs

13

are crying out for in countries which at the crucial time happen to be less fortunate (although not necessarily economically so). What could be more innocuous than chocolates, cigarettes, whisky, nylon stockings and the like? Items whose simplicity would seem laughable today. Would you believe that my father did good business for ten years on the China coast smuggling coal shovels!

The time will come when one cannot expect much more from life; that is the moment to start to write one's autobiography. If you have judged it nicely it should come out in print just before you enter the crematorium, or just after, if you so desire.

Among my earliest memories, possibly at six years of age, is that of a boat trip to rendezvous with a sailing ship at anchor. I remember my father in consultation with the shipmaster — the two captains meanwhile being served drinks by a white-coated steward who also gave me a glass. Had you been standing on the quay when we returned that evening, in the far-off twenties, you might have observed a heavily laden boat coming alongside. My father would off-load the goods in two handbags and deliver them to the house while an innocent six year old kept watch on the covering tarpaulin.

That was my introduction to smuggling. I shall follow this up later.

I have a lifelong memory of my first trading. During my explorations of my environment I had discovered a big old anchor and a few feet of chain on an islet some two kilometres from the pier. On a hot July forenoon I decided to do something about it and proceeded to 'borrow' a small boat. The oars had, of course, been removed, but I had made myself a paddle and after a laborious jaunt I began to load up the goods. The operation entailed blood, sweat and tears and a good deal of inventiveness. Triumphant, I toiled back to the pier where a small derrick facilitated unloading onto an — again — 'borrowed' hand-cart. Sweating it uphill to the scrap-iron dealer, I found his place closed for the hot hours of the day. I had then to park the cart in a safe place and proceed home for a delayed midday meal, soaking wet and exhausted.

At it again in the late afternoon, I at last met the old man and could offer my merchandise. He confronted me with an air of assumed indifference which also implied the idea of theft. He could, albeit reluctantly, accept the anchor and chain for one red penny (NKr 0.07 in the early twenties). I took comfort in the thought that 'the receiver is as bad as the thief'. With a lump in my throat I made a fine show and told him: 'All right, you have a deal.'

This was the first of two experiences with old anchors; the second will be related later.

I made a fair profit, however, in my other ventures, among other things collecting and selling empty bottles, scrap metal, rags and hessian sacks.

I had to admire my parents on Sunday morning when I met them in the much frequented street on the way to Church. I had a sack of empty bottles from the morning's collection on my shoulder and my appearance was not of the best. Not at all nonplussed, they simply ignored me.

I must also mention an anecdote which was repeatedly quoted by the old folk when they met me: 'Do you remember the old man in the boat who could not get his motor started?' They were referring to an occasion, long since forgotten by me, when at six or seven years of age I am reported to have stood at the quay with my younger brother watching a man trying to crank his motor into life.

'Have you opened the cock on the gas tank?' queried the six year old.

'Of course,' came the disgruntled reply.

'Have you given the motor a "wetter"?'

'Naturally,' he wheezed, wiping his brow on his forearm.

'Oiled and greased properly, and opened for cooling water?' pressed the precocious questioner.

The old man, now manifestly annoyed and with laboured breath, made a painful effort to straighten his back and get a closer look at the source of this irritating examination. 'U-huh,' he said.

'So swing like the devil!' * came the crisp order, whereupon the motor roared to life.

Thus Captain Wilson at the age of seven!

Regardless of my feelings on the subject, I was put into a private school the same year. It was Mrs Bryn's Preparatory School, which catered for boys and girls. The benefit of a year

---

* 'Så sveiv som bare faen' — literally: Crank like hell!

there was that one was able to start in the second class at the Primary School. I finished this schooling more than a year earlier than the children who commenced at the prescribed time, and my thoughts were already directed towards going to sea.

As far as my father was concerned, going to sea before the age of fourteen or fifteen was quite out of the question. He insisted I first take the three year secondary school course and then I could decide on the sea. He was adamant and I had no choice but to agree.

At the end of secondary schooling I took the exams and without waiting for the results (which were disappointing anyway) I signed on a deckboy on one of my father's ships. They were not large vessels and traded only in the North Sea and Baltic ports, with occasional voyages to the Mediterranean. A few months of this life served only to whet my appetite for wider horizons. I signed off in Antwerp and joined a newer vessel, the *Ravnaas*. She was 7.500 DWT, large for her time, and my first trip was to Canada in ballast to load newspaper rolls at Port Alfred in the St Lawrence River.

My first taste of the Atlantic was not very encouraging. In fact, I was still horribly seasick. After leaving Canada *en route* for New York, my seasickness, compounded by homesickness, made me beg the bosun to help me find a homeward-bound vessel. On arrival in New York I thought I would take the first opportunity to work my passage home. I had had enough of the sea. The bosun promised to do what he could and I felt somewhat relieved.

By the time we reached New York my sickness had vanished and I went ashore in high spirits. This was during the Prohibition, and I remember seeing a bottle of Coca-Cola for the first time, having only heard of it previously from my shipmates. We were in a bar in Brooklyn when the barman suddenly produced *beer*. A little later and equally unexpectedly, a policeman turned up.

'My God!' I choked into my beer, 'We'll end up in the clink.' I had visions of Alcatraz, Sing-Sing, and the less salubrious State Penitentiaries I had heard so much of.

'Don't worry,' said a shipmate, nodding in the direction of the representative of the law. 'That man has been bribed by the bar-owner, so nothing will happen. That's the way they do things over here.'

After discharging in New York we made a ballast trip down to La Plata. Included in our provisions taken aboard in New York was catfish, which I now tasted for the first time and found very agreeable. At La Plata we sailed up the river to St Nicolas and St Lorenzo for a part cargo of Indian corn: maize. During this trip I witnessed a locust swarm. For several hours the sky was blackened by these voracious creatures, and when settling down they devoured everything and laid waste enormous tracts of land in their unchecked progress from horizon to horizon.

In port I was made nightwatch, which meant I simply slept at night, turned out the crew at six in the morning and, of course, swept up the locusts from the decks. I was then free to go ashore and see the sights, mostly primitive pubs and half wild gauchos.

After loading, which took a long time, we shifted down to Buenos Aires for loading to capacity; this was because of the shallow depth of water in the river. It was here I first visited a brothel, after getting myself suitably inebriated.

In the 1930's the crewmen could not afford to drink ashore, and they bought something called *alcohol puro* which they smuggled on board. Using sugar and water heated over kerosene lamps (the electricity was turned off at eight each evening) they managed to produce a very potent drink. Its effect on them sent me scurrying to safety — they could be a very wild bunch at times. Otherwise a cheap drink ashore was called *Ca a*: a name probably derived from sugarcane.

After what seemed an age at sea we finally arrived at Las Palmas, in the Canary Islands — while it was my unenviable task to pick rust below during my watch. The bum-boats surrounded us in the usual way and their crews were quickly on board with all their wares laid out on the hatches. The excitement was too much for me and I sneaked up to the deck more than once just to see what was going on.

When at last my four hour watch was over I went on deck and it was not long before I had bartered my home-knitted woollen stockings and other such comforts for a small white dog. I also bought a stem of Canary bananas and to this day I can remember how wonderful they tasted.

The little dog was quite devoted to me and I thought it the most beautiful creature I had ever seen. However, the bosun came up with the ominous news that though he had often seen these dogs brought on board, they had never survived the rigours of sea life. I suspected him of being in collusion with the captain who came along later and tried unsuccessfully to buy the dog from me at many times the original value. But I loved it and would not sell at any price. A few days later it took sick and quickly died and a crewman did me the favour of dumping it overboard. So ended my first experience with dogs — by no means my last. It was a voyage which gave me many first experiences.

We discharged I remember in Belfast, Ireland, and after many similar voyages I signed off and went home. I had been with the ship for one and a half years and was now nearing eighteen years of age.

After a short holiday my thoughts turned to the idea of joining one of the big sailing vessels operating out of Mariehamn, Aland, but my father, an old sailing-ship man himself, sabotaged any such an idea. It would be better, he said, to take a six-month break at Otto Treider's Mercantile School in Oslo and then decide. Whereupon he installed me in a small *pension* in the capital where I met others from my home town and I came through the complete course better equipped for my master's career in shipping.

I had now abandoned the idea of Finland, and for a time worked at my father's office. City life began to appeal to me — especially girls . . . . Small wonder I was tempted to continue this lazy existence but I needed more sea-time; forty-eight months were necessary for entry to the Maritime Academy for Chief Officers, Masters and Extra-Masters. However, in 1938, I took over my father's office with the two ships he had running all through the years of the great Depression.

When civil war broke out in Spain and Mussolini subsequently invaded Abyssinia (now Ethiopia) the office was under constant threat from the banks. We had piled up an enormous stack of unpaid bills and each Christmas the bank threatened to bring the ships home in the New Year and bankrupt us. It was a very heavy strain on my father, in fact it drove him to an early grave. He died in June 1940, after the German occupation of Norway, after managing to keep the ships going throughout the bleak thirties when many shipping companies simply folded up. The threat of the dole, the support of his wife and three children and the running of the company proved a burden more than his stout heart could bear.

At the time in 1939 when war finally became a reality, I was hunting in the country with friends. Norway was neutral then and like many others we saw no reason to interrupt our holiday. The first news I received was that a ship had been torpedoed and sunk by the Germans: she was the *Solaas* and her owner was my father. He had had her and a sister ship, the *Stensaas*, built in 1917 and she had been launched by my mother. He bought both ships back at the start of the thirties for sentimental reasons. There was no loss of life and the crew all got to Denmark safely in the lifeboats.

My father and I were so attached to one another that our relationship became more one of 'boys together' than anything else. He told me about his life and I was always a good listener. Finally, before he died, he gave me some papers — the truth of a story which had gnawed at his heart for many years, and I believe it proper to reproduce it in English later on in this account.

My father trusted me implicitly. In the early days, even before I had reached the age of eighteen, he decided to change the company name from John Wilson Ltd. to John Wilson & Son Ltd., and the stationery was changed accordingly. He then set about buying out the shareholders. They were few in number: an English ship-chandler, an English shipbroker, an Oslo shipbroker and a few friends in Arendal. The shares themselves were almost worthless since the company was virtually bankrupt at the time, so he acquired the stock for a relatively small outlay. He managed to find some money which he had salted away somewhere and on which we were living during the Depression in the 1930's.

Now sole owner of the company, he transferred it to me at my request, but not without some misgivings. 'You now own everything, boy,' he said. 'I don't like it, but it is what you want and I must take the chance. Remember, you now have the power to throw me out into the street.'

I thought this was marvellous, a demonstration of his absolute faith in me, and with all the optimism of youth I thought I would have no problem in coping with the standards he set me. He was a shrewd man, prepared to gamble on a son he was close to. I was not to know that the burden he bore for so long was soon to put him in his grave.

Our attachment was such that he would deny me nothing, even taking a drink with me, invariably Scotch whisky and soda, and talking the night away. He would turn a blind eye to my many misdemeanours or would bring them out into the open — and drink for one so young would today be regarded as a misdemeanour. He never mentioned the incident when as a small boy of six I had borrowed the family boat. Another time I got a little drunk and smashed up the family car, yet this too he took with his usual forbearance and stoic optimism. Once a party with girls on the boat got a little out of hand and the boat caught fire; we had to sink it to dowse the flames — again not a word of reprimand.

Mother, of course, was different. She would pass the whole tale of woe over the telephone to my brother, her favourite, who was then serving as an officer at a military academy, and he would then recount it to me later with many a laugh. 'That horrible boy!' she exclaimed. 'First he has smashed up the car so it won't be available for months and now he has ruined the boat so we have to spend the whole summer sitting in the garden!'

I shall, however, here and now express my devotion to and admiration for my mother and also give her full credit for her exceptional loveliness. A loyal, homely and faithful wife and mother, always undemanding; she took the fat with the lean. Invariably she supported my father whom she outlived by thirty-three years.

I am rather inclined to identify myself with Ibsen's Peer Gynt as I literally spirited her into 'The abode of Peace' at the age of ninety-seven plus. The last afternoon — she had had her usual glass of port wine — I believe bore a resemblance to the death scene of Peer's mother, Aase:

'. . . and I can depart in peace.'

'Why! What are you saying?'

'Aye, all will soon be over. When you see that my eyes are glazing, you must close them carefully.'

'Nay, now we will chat and forget what is awry and crooked. You were ever a kindly soul. Mother! I see a sparkling and gleaming afar now; outside stands St Peter and prays you to enter in.'

'Lord, Lord, shall we two come together? I will lie back and close my eyes then, and trust to you, my boy.'

A wonderful thing is a mother — the only wrong she ever does you is to die and leave you. I can only add: 'Forgive me for the ill I have done you.'

As already mentioned, in those far off days my father left with me a set of papers which he had prepared in his elegant longhand. They dealt with the beginnings of the company John Wilson Ltd. and relate how during the First World War, after many years of serving under sail and steam, he decided to start for himself. After about a year ashore, he managed to enlist the services and partnership of a bookkeeper at the firm of Boe & Son. This man, Mørland, also had the necessary knowledge of commercial practice and general clerical routine; and thus it was that the firm of Wilson & Mørland came into existence.

They began with some old ships which my father bought up cheaply and put into service. This turned out to be a highly successful venture and led them to having two ships built in Denmark, the steamships *Solaas* and *Stensaas* which my mother launched in 1916. It was some time after this that he wrote the testimony earlier referred to and which is reproduced hereafter.

What is this document? How can it be assessed?

It is a cry from the heart of a man at the end of his days; a man who could have indulged himself in far far more formidable terminology, at the same time unleashing a flood of bitterness to relieve the torture that must have been gnawing at his heart until his dying breath. But he had nothing to gain, and nothing more to lose by committing his thoughts to paper.

Life is all chance and risk, yet few would knowingly swim in shark-infested waters as he did, diving in head-first and swimming alongside them for as long as they allowed him, until their insatiable appetites caused them to turn . . . . The long years that have laid their dust over this message from the grave have done nothing to diminish its poignancy, or its warning.

Is the world of business very much different today, I wonder? Speaking for myself on this matter I can only say that I personally have no axe to grind. These anecdotes which came echoing down the years from a period during the First World War which was remarkable for its reckless speculation, should be recorded, if only for historical rather than hysterical purposes. All the main characters have left the scene and my relationship with their descendants are as cordial as they are untarnished.

A quasi scribe, Birger Dannevig, framed a kind of commemorative booklet for the shipowning firm Mørland. Incidentally, the same individual once, in my prolonged absence with Barquentine *Regina Maris*, wrote an article in the local newspaper accusing me of having seduced the crew to sail under false colours and had thus incurred a term in jail. When I received the article I wrote to the newspaper, and being an unblemished National, my article stuck in his gorge to a degree that he was silenced ever after. The glasshouse in which we are dwelling compels us to refrain from the amusement of throwing stones — he took French leave . . . but . . . omittance is no quittance. The booklet which he framed for Mørland contains the very silly statement: Mørland decided to start his own company — which was registered under the style of Wilson and Mørland.

2

The Testimony Of Captain John Wilson

John Wilson
Managing Owner 1916--1918.

Arnt J. Mørland
Managing Owner 1916---1957.

In May 1915 I returned home to Arendal from the sea. In the meantime, however, Boe had sold off all the ships in St Olaf Shipping Co. and I was thus without employment. I thought about starting myself in shipping but came to the conclusion that I needed a partner. I decided on Arnt J. Mørland who worked in Boe's office. Boe had no great need for him any longer as they only had *S/S Nedenes* left from their fleet. I visited Mørland again and again in order to persuade him to join me in starting a company but he did not have the courage. I did not give up however, and after working on him and pressing him for more than a year, he finally capitulated. Thus the Agdesiden Shipping Co., was born in September 1916.

Initially we decided to take Kr 100,000 of shares in the company ourselves, but then decided to increase this amount to Kr 200,000, as the bank was very positive in view of the fact that thesubscription surpassed our expectations. Finally, the bank agreed to us taking a share in the company of Kr 400,000. (This as Mørland's idea. I was against it but Mørland argued that if anything did go wrong, then we were no worse off with Kr 400,000 than with Kr 200,000. We would be ruined anyway.)

The value of the shares went down instead of up as we had hoped. Mørland and I were in an uncomfortable position with the bank and felt the pressure quite badly.

At the constituent assembly Mørland and I were unanimously granted two per cent of the purchase price of the company's ship as founders' rewards. We valued this at Kr 85,000 but were immediately met with protests from shareholders who had not been present at the general constituent assembly and who demanded that we should repay this amount. If we were forced to do this we would not be able to fulfil our commitments to the bank.

The old consul, Chr. Th. Boe, knew, of course, all about our business affairs and offered to try to help us out of the situation. One day he came up to the office and said that he was sure that he had heard that the bank would be willing to value the Agdesiden shares at fifty per cent and claim repayment on this basis — i.e., as far as we were concerned a payment of Kr 200,000. Mørland and I would have been able to manage this.

Consul Boe had everything planned. When he saw that his arrows had hit home and had the required effect he adopted a patronizing tone, saying that he did not want to see Mørland and myself ruined — he had been extremely satisfied with me as captain and with Mørland as clerk in the years we had been with him and he felt he had to help us out of this difficulty. Whereupon he offered to take over all the shares at par value on condition, naturally, that he took over control of the company — Mørland should return to Boe's office in his previous capacity and I was to become inspector for all the ships.

We were so depressed that this villainous suggestion from Boe seemed like a liberation and we agreed at once. The next day, however, when we realized properly what we were losing and saying goodbye to, we were sick with despair. I asked Mørland to go and see Hammer the bank manager. He did this straight away and told him what he had heard about the bank's plans. On hearing this, Hammer flew into a rage, saying that it was all a pack of lies and that no repayment would be demanded. So when Mørland returned and we realized the nature of Boe's move to sink us, we decided to go up and talk with him. By then, however, he had already gone in to Kristiania together with his henchman Ole Schrøder in order to strike while the iron was hot.

Mørland and I hurried after and found Boe at the Grand Hotel. We made our suggestion and asked Boe to help us so that we could retain control of the company we had started but no — he was as hard as flint, flew into a rage and threatened us, saying that if we did not willingly hand over control to him he had power enough behind him to ensure that he could take over the company anyway.

So there was nothing we could do about the obstinate old scoundrel. We went down to Bredal the lawyer to ask for advice and obtain his opinion on whether the concession we had received from a unanimous constituent assembly could be reversed. After having conferred with his partners he stated that no one could reverse this decision. This made us look more on the bright side of things and we returned home to await developments at the extraordinary general meeting which had already been announced.

The time of the meeting arrived and all were present. After it had been announced that Wilson and Mørland had asked to be relieved of their control of the company and that it had been recommended that Chr. Th. Boe & Son be elected in their place, high court Attorney P.A. Pedersen took the rostrum and protested in the strongest possible manner against this. On behalf of himself and all the shareholders whom he represented he insisted that Wilson and Mørland should remain in control and that we should retain the concession we had received in the form of founders' rewards. High court Attorney Pedersen also spoke out strongly against Chr. Th. Boe and called him an outright scoundrel, saying that if he (Boe) did obtain control of the company, he would eat it all up, right down to the last crumb.

Petter Lund Boe and the son, Christian Boe, were present and were witness to all of this storming and raging, but made no attempt to answer back or make Attorney Pedersen in any way answerable for his statements.

Meanwhile, the result of this meeting was that Wilson and Mørland received a unanimous vote of confidence and remained in control of the company.

Mørland and I had been trying to sell the shipbuilding contracts in Frederikshavn for some time and had kept the price at Kr 3,300,000 or thereabouts. As we had agreed in the meantime to Boe's suggestion about passing control over to him, he felt so sure of himself that he had begun to negotiate the sale of the Frederikshavn contracts with C.K. Hansen in Copenhagen at a price of Kr 2,800,000 without the knowledge of Mørland and myself. We got to know about this through a letter from C.K. Hansen to Boe which was sent to us by mistake. If Boe had obtained control previously he would have sold the Frederikshavn contracts for Kr 2,800,000 — or even below this price — and then purchased one or two large vessels or contracts at unprecedentedly high prices, thus taking advantage of the situation himself.

He had attempted to redeem himself by stating that the company had been taken over by him in such a chaotic condition that nothing more could have been done. My suspicions are based on extremely reliable sources: a conversation with Ole Schrøder revealed to me all of the plans of the Boe plot.

As can be seen, Boe did not achieve his aim this time, in spite of all his intrigues and dirty tricks. Nevertheless Captain N.P. Larsen warned me not to be too confident — he said that he knew Boe and thought that he would be back again on a different tack.

Some time later Petter L. Boe, the then chairman of the board of the Agdesiden Shipping Co., died. We, Mørland and I, together with the other directors, Attorney Ove Andersen (totally Boe's man), Ole Schrøder, and Hammer, the bank manager, all agreed that it must have been a severe blow to old Boe to lose his son. He had been the only one who could have taken over Boe's business when old Boe died — and he could pass away at any time, being over eighty years old.

To give old Boe some encouragement we agreed to offer him the chairmanship of the board after his son and Boe accepted this with pleasure. This we should never have done, but who could have known that a man on the edge of the grave could have been so steeped in malice?

Far from keeling over after the blow of losing his son, Boe regained his vitality instead. He was always extremely friendly to me and really gave the impression that he meant well. Now as I write this and think more carefully about Boe's friendliness, and at the same time think a bit more carefully about the relationship between Mørland and Boe and how it developed, I realize that these two had been deceiving me behind my back.

Boe and Mørland still held conferences in Boe's favourite — amongst other things he was elected to the board of A/S Nedenes and, as I have said, he was always to be found together with Boe.

At the time I attached no importance to this, but now I can see what kind of people Mørland 'the religious' and Boe were. I was out travelling a lot for the company and was always busy with inspections of the shipbuilding in Frederikshavn, so Boe and Mørland had plenty of opportunity to work behind my back and lay their plans. However, I speeded up the work on the ships as much as I could and it transpired that I managed to achieve what I was working for.

As soon as I arrived in Frederikshavn I saw that the yard had all the power and could attribute any delays to acts of God. I knew that here I would have to work diplomatically.

For the sake of brevity, suffice it to say that my first move was to make friends with the director of the yard; this accomplished, I used my own way of furthering my plans which, it is fair to say, saved a lot of money for the company.

Director Mygind was up in Arendal after we had got the ships out of Denmark and wanted guarantees that they would not sail in the service of countries or in territorial waters which might be directly or indirectly advantageous to the enemies of Germany. Otherwise Germany would halt all supplies of materials to the yard. Naturally we refused to give such a guarantee. The director of the yard realized that having acquired the ships we were not obliged to give any further guarantees than had already been given and he stated in the presence of my wife that had it not been for me the vessels would not have been finished and delivered so quickly. Had Mørland been the one to negotiate with the yard, the ships would still have been hung up in dock at that time (summer 1918). Those were his very words.

The reason was that Mørland had adopted a very haughty attitude the one time he had been down there, and done damage which had taken me quite some time to put right. The reason for Mørland's behaviour with the yard was that he was anything but a man of the world. His sudden rise from being just 'Arnt' with Boe to being able to introduce himself as shipowner had gone to his head.

When we had got both of the ships out of Denmark everything looked much brighter for us. We placed the ships on routes we were entitled to according to the clauses of the contract and everything went quite well. Mørland, however, started behaving differently towards me — he was not the man he had been. It was as if he were hiding something from me.

In the early autumn or to be more exact, in the late summer of 1918, I began to feel poorly and started coughing. I paid a visit to Dr Høyer, who examined me and diagnosed a serious case of bronchitis. Høyer advised me to take a trip up into the country but I did not like the idea and remained at home taking my medicine. Rather than getting better, it got worse and with the autumn came the Spanish influenza. Mørland fell ill and had to stay at home, as did Christensen. The only ones left were Melby, the boy, and myself. I took on everything and as we were not so busy and my bronchitis worsened so that I felt really ill, I took the office work home with me so as not to have to go out in the raw autumn air. Melby fetched the post for me and stayed at the office.

Mørland was in bed at home with the Spanish influenza —

or so he said. Anyway, it must have been a light attack, as he was up and about again within about fourteen days. But that was his business. I stayed indoors, however, until Christmas week and even then Dr Høyer forbade me to go out but, after what I am about to describe, I was too afraid to stay inside and had to get out.

When Mørland had recovered from his illness he travelled to Kristiania a few times and on his return telephoned me and asked me to come down to the office as there was something he wanted to discuss with me. I said that I was unable to go out and was unlikely to do so before Christmas but that if it was important he could come up to me. He came a few days later and was very pleasant indeed. He sat for a long time, unable to carry out his villainous errand, but eventually out it came. His words were these:

'Yes, Wilson, I have been very sick — at death's door, right over the threshold — and I have been able to see all the evil things in this world which I had prepared myself to leave. When I had recovered and the danger was past my first thought, my first decision, was to renounce all of my business and devote myself totally to the Lord. In the meantime, however, I have pondered more over this, but, Wilson, you know that I cannot live from that. Now there is only one thing to do — you and I are so different. You are godless — you blaspheme and swear and several of my fellow believers have said that they do not understand how I can sit together with such a godless person as you. Indeed they have said that I could damage my soul by associating with you and talking to you every day. So I thought we might go our own ways in a spirit of friendliness.'

I answered that he could go if he wanted, leaving me to take over the company.

'Oh no, Wilson, you cannot do that — you've never had anything to do with the office — you cannot manage all that.'

I replied, 'Oh yes Mørland, I think I am much better at running a shipping company than you are and, as for office work, I can find a man to do that for me — after all that is the least of it and has nothing to do with the actual running of the company.' At this point Mørland says that he has spoken to the board and that he is sure of their votes.

'I see,' say I. 'So you have been working on this for a long time — you have gone behind my back — you are indeed a fine man.'

I then asked him to state his suggestion in full.

Well, I was to receive three years of profits without doing anything myself. Fifty per cent the first year and twenty-five per cent the other two. In addition, I was to have the full commission from the shipbuilding in England and moreover all of the gratuity I received from the yard in Frederikshavn. With that he thought I should be fully satisfied. I then asked him to leave, saying we should let things rest until I was well. I had not the energy for more at that point.

This set me back seriously in my sickness and as I was careless enough to tell everything to Aagot she received a blow which was a hair's breadth from costing her her life — at the time she was pregnant with Sigfried.

So a few weeks later Mørland was on the telephone again pushing and pressing me as if he were possessed. I decided, in spite of Dr Høyer, to go down and talk to Boe to find out whether he was part of this shameful game. Less than a minute of conversation with Boe made everything clear. I remonstrated with Boe on the shamefulness of this action against myself, the founder of the company. I asked Boe to do his part in getting things straightened out so that Mørland and I would not need to separate, as we had never had any disagreement. But Boe, the old scoundrel, was as hard as flint and would hear of no other arrangement. At this point I went to Attorney Olsen — but that was just a waste of time.

So Mørland and I began to negotiate. I tried to drag it out as long as possible in order to gain time as I still hoped that Mørland would realize what a shameful trick he was playing on me, but it was all to no avail. So I promised to abide by the terms of the separation stated above and said that when he had transferred the sterling amount with A.O. Andersen (the commission from the shipbuilding in England) to me and I had possession of the bank book, I would sign the agreement. Mørland then telephoned to A.O. Andersen and asked him to send the bank book in my name with the stated sterling amount and the book arrived the next day. I was still trying to delay things and demanded more stringent conditions, right up to the point where Mørland and I completely lost our tempers. Mørland said that he would agree to nothing more than three years' compensation and that he would find other ways of achieving his ends.

Before continuing, I must go back a little in time. When Mørland and I had been together for some time he began asking whether we could not earn a lot of money on repairs and shipwrecks and the like, and he thought that I, having been a captain, would know all about this. I said that with all the repairs and suchlike it was the custom that there was a gratuity for the captain and the inspector and that I would make sure that we obtained what we were entitled to. Mørland said that *I* could claim all of this and that *I* would give him *his* half share in the form of a present as we did not want to enter that kind of thing in the books. As you wish, I said, but one commission is just like any other in my opinion.

The first commission, and the others mentioned, we obtained when we tied up the final details on the Frederikshavn ships. Before leaving to tie things up, I asked Mørland whether I should see if there was anything to be had and, if so, what we should do with the money. Mørland asked me to do my utmost to obtain a good gratuity, saying that now we would see how deep the roots of friendship went between myself and the Danes. As I have said, he really pressed for me to obtain a good bonus. He could have *his* share as a present from me either to help buy a house or for something else.

When I closed the business in Frederikshavn I received Kr 4,000 for each ship, ie, Kr 4,000 for Mørland and the same for me. I deposited the amounts at Centralbanken in their respective bank books. When I returned Mørland was very inquisitive but I said that he should stop asking and that he could have his present whenever he wanted to buy something.

Mørland was living in Konigshavn in the summer of 1918 and a small house came up for sale which he wanted to buy. However, one day when I was down to visit him he said he did not think he should pay more than Kr 8,000 for it. He showed me the house and I said that he could buy it as I would be able to cover the balance which was roughly the amount standing in his name at Centralbanken. We agreed, therefore, that I should buy the house for him and draw from the above mentioned commission to pay for it. In the meantime the seller of the house withdrew and Mørland's share of the commission remained where it was. The amount was not discussed any further apart from the fact that it could remain at the bank until he bought a house in town.

Now we shall return to where I interrupted the negotiations between Mørland and myself about the conditions of separation.

As I said, we both lost our tempers and I said that I would go in to Kristiania to see what ought to be done. I also said to Mørland that we could dissolve the firm of Wilson & Mørland and inform the shareholders of this so that they could elect a new managing director — because as soon as *W & M* was dissolved the company would have no legally employed director — the bye-laws specifically stated that *the firm of Wilson & Mørland* was to be managing director of the company. At this Mørland paled, saying that if I were to do this there would be no compensation for me and that in all probability he would be elected, as he had the whole board on his side.

At this point we went up to Attorney Andersen and there we met Boe. Mørland and I started arguing and Mørland proceeded to explain in a distorted and untruthful way about the commission from Frederikshavn. He said amongst other things that he was never able to find out exactly how large the amount was and he himself had travelled in to Kristiania to see the bank — as I have said, he was lying; lying when it was to his advantage.

I asked to speak and explained the whole of our relationship with respect to our agreement about the commission — about the house which Mørland had wanted to buy — in other words everything. He neither could nor dared deny all of this but was shameless enough to claim that it had always been his intention to credit his share to the company — again lies.

I felt very sick and ill at ease about all of this. Limp and wretched as I was, I made no attempt to argue and signed the agreement. Thinking back on everything, I do not think I could have been in my right senses, the way I allowed myself to be shut out in that shameful way — without even the assistance of an Attorney. There they were, Boe and Mørland together, with their lawyer, Attorney Andersen, who was managing everything for them but gave the impression that he was only present as a member of the board and represented our interests equally. As I have said, it was all a plot hatched by Boe and Mørland, and Attorney Andersen, in his capacity as Boe's lawyer, of course had to support his client.

So I took out both bank boxes, Mørland's and my own — as I have described above, the commission was there at Centralbanken in each of the books — and said that if Mørland would credit his share to the company, then naturally, so would I, and showed the books to Boe and to Attorney Andersen. Then Mørland and I went back to our office and had the stated amounts transferred to Agdesiden Shipping Co.

Well, we had got so far, but the most difficult part still remained. This was to find a way of adequately pulling the wool over the shareholders' eyes with respect to the true state of affairs.

Attorney Andersen proceeded to prepare a circular to be sent to the registered shareholders. We were to insert a small, quite ordinary announcement so that no one would think anything was amiss, to the effect that I was leaving the company, which would continue as before. I pointed out to the attorney that by law the shareholders had to be informed *in detail* about what was to happen, and that the procedure he had in mind would conceal things from them. If they were then to find out about the real situation, there was a risk that they could cancel the whole of the decision at the general meeting and call for a new meeting. Attorney Andersen's reply was that there was no need to be so fussy, it would all work out — he did not believe that anyone would interfere.

For the sake of complete certainty, I was required to promise that if anyone at the general meeting should object to the dissolution of the firm Wilson & Mørland, then I would agree to the firm continuing to bear that name. This they also managed to include in my agreement with Mørland.

The circular letters were sent out and the general meeting was announced just like an ordinary annual general meeting. Proxies arrived just as they always did to our general meetings and sufficient proxies were present for a quorum. It cannot be left unsaid that there were only a very few — I think four or five — shareholders present. Apart from the directors themselves, all were from the town and surrounding district. The rest were proxies.

Old Boe chaired the meeting — he was chairman of the board — and everything was done so slyly that none of the shareholders present had any objections. It all went just the way the gentlemen had planned it. And as I, in accordance with the agreement, was bound not to try to ally myself with anyone else in the next three years in any attempt to take over the company, and had in fact undertaken to support Mørland, Boe and Mørland felt quite sure of themselves.

Many years have passed since I wrote this, and it had been my intention to present this description of events to a general meeting in order to let the meeting decide to what extent Mørland should be allowed to continue to represent the company as managing director. I sought advice from my cousin, Attorney J. Falck Andersen, about this, but he advised me against taking such a step, maintaining that I would achieve nothing other than revenge against Mørland. He would probably be dismissed as managing director and the company would be moved from Arendal to another town where the majority of shares was to be found. At the same time, however, my own reputation would suffer, even if it was only human to seek vengeance for such a villainous trick as Boe and Mørland had played. By doing that, I would be the cause of the company being taken away from the town.

So I left everything as it was.

Chr. M. Boe had counted on being able to take over the company himself if only he could get rid of me, but in the end he was not able to. Probably Mørland knew Boe's business too well from his time at the office there.

John Wilson

3

From My Memorandum Book

On 9th April 1940, the day of the invasion, my brother was serving in the army and I joined a volunteer resistance group in the mountains. After less than two weeks we had to submit in the face of far superior forces. Sigfried and I managed to hide away weapons and ammunition for the time which we knew would come, sooner or later, when the Allied forces would once again liberate Norway. The only things I kept at home were two pistols: a 6.25 and a 7.35 calibre, both hidden away at Arendal and later in Oslo.

After my father's death, I moved to Oslo with the office for the one remaining ship. I knew that everyone in Arendal would still consider me the 'unruly little lad', and any attempt to command respect among the elders of the town would be futile.

Our torpedoed ship had been rather poorly covered as regards insurance and the Germans had reduced the other to about a third. What proceeds I had, I put into real estate, which turned out to be a very good investment. With this and one operational ship, I needed a loan. I contacted my bank manager before I left Arendal. To my surprise, he arranged to meet me in the Grand Café, whereas I had expected to see him at his office. He treated me as the small-town boy — much to my disgust.

Having once established myself with an office in Oslo, I was fortunate in securing the services of a very clever chief clerk. The remaining ship, plus the real estate, an apartment house venture, now ran side-by-side until the second ship was torpedoed. Then, when the war ended, I sold the apartment house to buy a new ship.

During this period I made the acquaintance of a man who

was in business with a lawyer, who, I learned later, was a Nazi. He and his family had been members of the Quisling Party, NS, since its inception in 1933. Later he and his sister both served on the Eastern front — much dreaded even by the Germans themselves — and were both wounded and repatriated to Norway. It was through this firm that I acquired my apartment house, and in fact I actually shared an apartment with him for about a year. He discovered my pistols, and I learned a lot about him. He had been embezzling to such an extent that I was almost broke. Luckily, I found out in time, and threw him out after recouping what I could of the misappropriated funds — with which he had already launched a new venture. As a result of this, he went to the Germans.

I was engaged to be married and my fiancée was a girl from the North. On the eve of leaving for the North with my tailcoat in my suitcase and train ticket at the ready, I went out to meet my brother at a pre-arranged time. To my astonishment, he approached me flanked by four solid-looking characters whom I took to be soldier friends. But they were Quisling police, and I was at once arrested and taken to the station for questioning.

'Don't try to lie to us. Do you have any weapons?'

I knew at once who it was that had got me into this situation, and that it would be useless to try to deceive the questioner.

'Yes,' I said. 'I have two pistols which I've owned since before the Occupation.' I was trying to keep as cool as possible and check the rising panic in my breast (I had also hidden a cache of weapons in the mountains).

'And where are those pistols now?' Unflinching eyes held mine as a stoat transfixes a rabbit.

'I have them hidden in a wall outside a churchyard.'

'All right,' they said, 'let's go and find them, shall we?'

We drove out in one of their cars to where I hoped desperately was the correct spot. With trembling fingers I clawed away the loose brick in the wall, and with some relief brought to light the two wrapped pistols and a quantity of ammunition.

'Do you have anything else?'

'No.'

'This is all?'

'Absolutely.'

After further interrogation at their headquarters I was taken to the Norwegian prison in Aakebergveien, which bore the nickname 'Bayeren'.

My first experience there was being called at six am with a cup of weak coffee and some bread.

'This will cost you one krone *,' the man said.

I had a few coins in my pocket, and paid up — a gesture which was greeted by roars of laughter from the old lags in the corridor.

When the warden arrived at lunch-time I was able to button-hole him with a serious question. 'What will happen to me?' I was naturally very apprehensive. The Occupation was only a few months old and I was one of the first to be 'taken'. There were all kinds of posters in the streets warning about the consequences of hiding arms and the fate of would-be resisters and saboteurs.

'Well,' he said, 'it's either life-imprisonment or the firing squad. There is nothing less than "life", but usually they shoot them.'

My lunch turned to chalk in my mouth.

After two months at Bayeren, I was taken to the German prison which was in Moellergaten 19. This was a terrible experience which lasted some months. There were people there from some of the south coast towns, including Arendal, with whom I was acquainted. They had been involved in an important case, and could expect a serious judgement.

One old friend from Arendal had been imprisoned since the start of the Occupation, and was, like several others I knew, destined to spend the entire war in internment in various camps throughout Germany. Seeing their Jewish friends taken away to the gas chambers and the bestial treatment handed out by the Gestapo had a shattering effect on the nerves of the internees, with the result that, when they returned home, they were simply unable to face up to everyday life without the support of alcohol, which drove many of them to an early grave.

I can remember seeing tracks of blood along the passages leading to the bathrooms — the sign of a prisoner being dragged from a Gestapo 'treatment room'. I realized how lucky I was to be caught so early. In the euphoria induced by the swift occupation and easy conquest of several countries which took

---

* About ten pence.

them to the heart of Russia, the Germans were leniently disposed towards the pathetic first-offenders.

When my turn came for judgement at the Court Martial, I stood at attention before a long table at which sat a number of high-ranking officers, decorated like Christmas trees. They were in high spirits. After all, were they not on the brink of world domination, or at the very least the conquest of Europe? I was given a defence lawyer and at the end of the proceedings the prosecution took into account my youth and the fact that this was a first offence. They pressed for four years' hard labour, but my defence lawyer, whom I thought extremely good, managed to get this reduced to one year in addition to the six months which I had already spent in prison. But hard labour prisons had been abandoned in Norway one hundred years earlier. I would have to be transported to the 'Fatherland'.

After two weeks back in my cell I was transferred to Akershus Fort, then doing service as an abominable prison. My cell at the top of the building was nothing more or less than an oven. The terrific heat of mid-summer burned down through the roof, where, through a sky-light, I could peep out on the city of Oslo. A rusty bucket served for a toilet, and a half hour's march round the courtyard was all the exercise and fresh air we were allowed. Here we could see the other prisoners, many of whom were Germans who had fallen foul of their own strict laws.

My ugliest memory of this place was being called out in the middle of the night to witness prisoners taken away for capital punishment. This was deeply nerve-racking, and had serious effects on many of the witnesses — as indeed it was meant to have. I now began to look forward to transportation to Germany, but some civil case, the subject of which I cannot now recall, was still in abeyance, and had to be dealt with first.

I got permission through my lawyer to leave the prison and attend the hearings. I was accompanied by a German officer who appeared to be a personable type with a very accommodating manner. When the business of the court was concluded and we were returning to the prison, I was prompted to ask him if I could drop into my office *en route* and have a drink. To my surprise, he agreed, and we both went to the office, where I had a bottle of rum. I asked him one more favour: would he let me ring my mother and brother and invite them to a good restaurant for dinner, where he himself could be a guest. The dinner was a memorable reunion, and we wanted more time to talk together. I asked the guard if I could treat him to a haircut and shampoo in the hotel's basement, and this he readily agreed to, with a manicure and facial massage thrown in. But eventually it all had to end and we had to go back to the prison. On our way I met an old friend who offered me a packet of food — he knew the conditions in Akershus — and my guard allowed me to accept it.

Eight days later I had once again to go to the civil court, but this time things were very different. I had as guard a genuine example of Hitler's Gestapo. He began by giving me a little lecture. Producing a revolver from his breast pocket, he said, 'If you do anything untoward, I shall shoot you on the spot, and I am an expert. This is not going to be like your last trip. We know all about that fellow. He has been demoted and given a long prison sentence in Germany.'

This guard was undoubtedly a sadistic type, perverse, possibly psychopathic — and at the very least abnormal. He had the most frightening face I had ever seen — one which could freeze anyone he met. My affairs were quickly sorted out and I was marched straight back to my cell. As it turned out, this was the day I should have joined a contingent of some forty-five Norwegian prisoners for transportation to Germany. Some would be serving perhaps four years and others, like myself, shorter sentences. I had learned early in my prison career not to ask why another prisoner was being punished.

I was now delayed a further week and then put aboard a large ship destined for Denmark, where we would entrain for various concentration camps or prisons throughout Germany. This time, however, there were only four Norwegians, together with about thirty Germans. We were stowed deep down in the hold, in bunks five tiers high. The other three Norwegians had sentences similar to mine. One, a member of a good diplomatic family, had been sentenced for stealing German souvenirs from restaurants and similar places. Another, an old farmer, was convicted of possessing an ancient shotgun which he had hanging at his farm and which he had undoubtedly overlooked. I never met any of them again.

We were put together with eight Germans with whom we got along very well, under the circumstances. We had no problem with their language, and we also ate together. Before the ship docked in Denmark we were issued with a parcel of food for twelve men: sausages, butter and bread. The Norwegians were to take care of it in their bags. On arrival at the station, the Germans were suddenly marched off onto one train and we to another, with the result that we were left with all of their rations. I felt sorry for those poor devils; we were so sure that we would all travel together to our final destination.

The train we were put on was jam-packed, with people standing and squatting in the corridors, but we were allocated a first class compartment together with our guards, two high-ranking German officers. During the twelve hour journey there was precious little rapport between us except when we began to take food. We observed that the Germans, though they had bread and sausage, were without butter, which we, needless to say, had in large quantity. We offered them some but the offer was curtly declined. I did notice that they had brought with them some salt herring and other delicacies, acquired in Norway for their families.

Our arrival in Hamburg at the stroke of midnight was greeted by the foreboding wail of air raid sirens. Within minutes the whole station area, which had been a sea of humanity, was deserted. Even our guards had taken refuge in one of the many air raid shelters, and we four Norwegian prisoners suddenly found ourselves alone. The prospect of Allied bombers overhead did not worry us for a moment.

The idea of escape entered my mind: it would not be difficult to slip over the border into Denmark, which, although also occupied, would be a stepping-stone into neutral Sweden. The thought had already occurred to me during the restaurant escapade in Oslo, but then as now the consequences were too awful to contemplate: the Germans would have taken my mother and brother, and brought to an end the shipping business for which my father had striven so hard. There would be nothing left to go back to. My three companions had similar fears, so we had to make do with the relative freedom we enjoyed while the air raid lasted. When the 'all clear' sounded and the area came to life again, we had the problem of trying to locate our guards! Finally reunited, we were taken to the local prison at Fuhlsbüttel, outside Hamburg. Here we stayed, in our civilian clothing, for two days, while the formalities for our entry into the hard labour prison were completed. Everything we owned, all our clothing and personal belongings, were taken away, and we were given prison uniforms, one for working days and one for Sundays. The uniforms were black with yellow stripes, and would have to do us in all conditions, together with square foot cloths. The latter were difficult to use because of the wooden clogs we had to wear. For underwear we had drawers which tied below the knee. As was only to be expected, many tall prisoners ended up with shirts which barely reached the navel, while shorter prisoners found their shirts hanging below their knees. This was what we had to wear when we stood to attention each night, our clothes folded on a stool outside the cell. A comical looking parade, to say the least.

There was an extraordinary mixture of people doing hard labour at this place. Some had been imprisoned in 1933 as communists; young idealists who looked like old men; a murderer doing forty-five years. There were homosexuals, perverts castrated for consorting with animals, a man doing seven years for associating with goat. I must say that to me he himself looked remarkably like a Satyr. There were also political prisoners and a number of gypsies. The place was so overcrowded that we had to live three to a cell intended for one. My two cell mates turned out to be good enough companions, but after a day or two we knew all there was to know about each other, with the result that we were soon in danger of boring each other to death. Many old lags preferred the solitary life.

I had a close shave one day. A German 'prisoner' approached me and casually and pleasantly asked me why I was in jail.

'Well, you know,' I answered, with the minimum of enthusiasm, 'I was in possession of weapons and the German police in Norway are very clever. They soon found out about them and I was given a year's hard labour.'

'Uh-huh,' he said cosily. 'Well, that is soon over. I guess when you are home again you will make contact with your friends in the resistance.'

The wrong word here would certainly have sealed my fate.

'No,' I replied. 'I have learned my lesson. I know where the best hope for Norway lies. In fact, when I get back I may join the Nazi party under our great leader "Quisling".'

'Will you really do that?' He seemed to see things in a new light.

'Certainly,' I said. 'I believe it's the only way for Norway.'

He withdrew. I had escaped the fangs of a most venomous snake.

We were now working on camouflaging at Fuhlsbüttel Airport in Hamburg. The whole building was covered with laths and hessian cloth on stages, to which trees and greenery were added to give the appearance of a wooded hillside. The guards on this assignment were amicably disposed and I found the time pleasant and the work interesting. Whenever I fly into Hamburg today I can still see the water tower and the prison buildings which I remember so well.

Two days before my time was up I was given back the clothing which had been taken away at the beginning of the sentence, and then sent to the ordinary prison. I was sorry to part with my two cell mates, who had a further three years to do, but I was now awaiting transportation back to Norway, and nothing could dampen my spirits. I was in possession of my release paper and wages, which amounted to six Reich marks.

I should mention here that it was during my sojourn as guest of the Germans that my ship *Stensaas* was torpedoed. That was in 1942. What became of the man who betrayed me I did not learn until the end of the war. He had continued to act as an informer for the Germans, and was no doubt well rewarded for his efforts, but when he ran out of names he began inventing them. He was soon found out and ended up in the gas chambers.

4

The New World

At the end of the war the Norwegian government began disposing of a fleet of German ships in compensation for war losses. Having previously got wind of this, I was first to put in an application. I had lost both my ships, the *Solaas* having been torpedoed even before hostilities began and the *Stensaas*, commandeered by the Germans, being torpedoed by the British. Things looked very black. After a long period of anxious waiting, I at last telephoned the distributing committee to hear what had become of my application. Imagine my disappointment when they told me the application could not be found! 'We are extremely sorry,' they said, 'but send us a new application. We still have a few ships left, one of which you can have.' I could hardly contain my anger and roundly accused them of underhand dealing, as what few old wrecks remained at this stage would have been worthless to me. I was asked to retract my accusation. I refused, nor would I send in another application. They insisted: I was adamant. I would 'hear more of this'. A report went to the Attorney General, thence to the Crown Prosecutor, and so to the police, and I was finally called in to give an explanation. I re-affirmed what I had said before, and insisted that it was up to them to prove that everything was indeed above board and that there was no villainy afoot. I had lost everything during the war, I had been denounced as a resistance fighter, I had spent eighteen months doing hard labour in Germany. Now I was to be denied the chance to rebuild my livelihood by people giving preference to friends with influence.

'Well,' said my interlocutor, 'you may be right. But if I were you, I should not try to take on the government in such a dispute.' And that was the end of it. There was I, expecting the wrath of the State to come down on my head, and nothing happened. All the papers appear to have been duly filed away and the whole case evaporated into thin air. I heard nothing more, but neither did I get a ship.

Through the good offices of a friend I contacted a man who had acquired two of the vessels and now wanted to sell one: a 5,000 ton coal-burning freighter, built in war-time Britain. His price was high and I had barely half the money. My lawyer, Rudolf Horn, a grand old gentleman and a Supreme Law Barrister, tried to dissuade me.

'Mr Wilson,' he said, 'this is too much to take on. You cannot manage it.'

'I can,' I insisted, 'and furthermore, I will. Let's go and see the bank manager and ask for a loan at once.'

Horn and I were in full agreement that this bank manager, Gude-Due of the Christiania Bank and Kreditkasse, was an unpleasant character.

'You can have this loan,' he said, 'and the interest will be six per cent per annum.'

That seemed on the high side at the time, and I timorously asked for a lower rate.

'Well, if you have any objection, you don't get a loan at all,' was his curt response.

Fortunately, the manager of the Norwegian Credit Bank was of an infinitely more accommodating disposition. Here I got complete satisfaction at one per cent lower interest. I went straight back to the Christiania Bank and Kreditkasse and told them I was transferring my account.

At last the ship was mine. I renamed her *Penelope* after the *Penelope Tutton*, a vessel of my grandfather's fleet in Swansea, Wales, in the 1870's. I could not afford to convert her to oil-burning, as was usual in those days, but sailed her on coal. I served on board during the summer holidays as Mate, and continued studying for my Master's Certificate.

I had great plans. There are risks in running a shipping business, and one needs luck, nerve and business acumen as well as seamanship. I lived in constant dread of seeing my assets eroded in taxes and duties and the like. I thought I might, at least initially, sail her under the Panamanian flag. I had now attained my Master's Certificate, and thought I would emigrate to America with my wife and family. It was only after I had made a lot of preparations for this move that I found out that it would take five years to obtain American citizenship. This was a blow, and called for a change of tactics.

I went to see the Honduran Consul and explained my scheme to establish myself in a country with more liberal tax laws and where private enterprise and initiative still meant something. He listened with interest. He could, he was sure, be of great assistance to me. I would take with me letters of introduction to many prominent people he had known and befriended over the years: lawyers, businessmen, even a foreign minister. I was elated.

I studied Spanish when I could, notwithstanding that my English still left much to be desired. A fourteen day crossing brought us to Cristobal in the Panama Canal Zone. I went to New York to draw some dollars and on my return we took the train to the capital, Panama. We installed ourselves at the Hotel International, which was only a few yards up the road from the station, and began the long quest for a Honduran passport.

I first travelled to Tegucigalpa to meet an influential businessman, carrying a letter of introduction from the Consul. My reception was decidedly cool. Yes, he had known and had dealings with the Consul, but that was a long time ago and they had lost contact over the years. Disappointed, I tried the law firm recommended by the Consul, one of the finest in Tegucigalpa.

I produced my letter of introduction to one of the directors and was told it would be in order. He would take 'the necessary steps'. It would take five years to obtain citizenship. With a heavy heart I returned to Panama with a bottle of whisky.

Time went on and the hotel bills grew. My furniture lay at the wharf. We had two children not yet out of nappies. I would be able to sell the furniture to get us out of trouble, at least until we were so deeply in debt that even this expedient would be denied us. We were not yet accustomed to the insufferable heat and much of our clothing was, of course, designed for northern latitudes.

One evening I saw an advertisement in the newspaper for an apartment in Bella Vista. My wife and I took a taxi to have a look at it. I at once rented the apartment from a family of Egyptian Jews who turned out to be very friendly and who later gave me invaluable assistance. The apartment was marvellous: clean and airy, with a tropical sitting room opening onto a balcony. In response to a request for a down payment, I gave the owner six months' rent in advance. He seemed pleased.

'Now,' I asked, 'can you help me get our luggage out of the customs down in the Canal Zone?'

'Do you have papers?'

'No.'

'*Madre mia!*' Hands and eyes flew heavenwards. 'I will go down and see what I can do.'

And he could do it. For the usual 'reward', the customs officials released our furniture without inspection.

I discussed my problem with the son of the house — the parents were leaving for Venezuela to expand their business — and mentioned the fact that it would take five years through the official channels to become a citizen of Honduras. Could he help me?

After some deliberation he gave me the name of a lawyer he was sure would be able to help me. I quickly located this man and at once things began to look up.

'Yes,' he said, 'I can fix that. You will have Honduran citizenship enabling you to travel on a Honduran passport, and also a Honduran Master's Certificate. All this will take a couple of months and will cost you $5,000.' I caught my breath. That was a lot of money in 1947. His English was poor, so he wrote it down for me to ensure there would be no mistake — and the figure he wrote was $4,000! I gave him $1,000 in advance and left him to get to work.

I had only two white suits, and needed to keep myself as smart as possible for all the visits to lawyers, banks, etc. The heat and travelling conditions on the buses made this rather difficult. As soon as I got back to the apartment, I would change into pyjamas and continue my studies in Spanish. One day, the lawyer came to visit. He seemed a little nervous — my guess is that he was not paying his contacts enough, and had probably been pocketing most of the money himself.

I managed to restore his equilibrium with a few drinks and, in fact, nothing untoward happened until later. On that occasion he probably got away with it by passing round a little more money. Three times a week I had to visit his office. I waited hours and hours, getting more and more nervous as time dragged on, and still nothing was forthcoming. I understood it was an extremely difficult assignment and we would just have to be patient. He told me that two years previously he would have been able to procure a passport for $200. Everything had been tightened up, and I had come at a most difficult time. At last there was news.

He now filled in a 'background' for me. I had come to Honduras with my father in the thirties. My father was a mining engineer and was looking for metals in the hills around Honduras. Being very young at the time, I could naturally remember very little about this. He had lived in tents or cheap hotels, and I knew little or nothing of his acquaintances. It was all so long ago . . . .

We needed half a dozen witnesses and travelled to the capital, Tegucigalpa in Honduras, for the swearing in, and our valiant lawyer again produced the goods. He picked up some of the most dreadful types you could find on the streets. They would swear to anything, on the Bible, of course, for a reasonable compensation. Admirable fellows they were: bleary eyes, dirty clothes, shoes open at the front, unshaven. The mere sight of them could set you scratching yourself. They began with rising voices and wild gesticulations that surely could only mean they were having some sort of bitter argument. My immediate thought was that the police would appear and cart us all off to the local clink. But then I realized that it was just their way of greeting each other, and the whole affair went swimmingly.

The day arrived when the lawyer procured a copy of the exam paper I would have to sit. All the questions were in Spanish, of course, and just as I was thinking that I did not have a snowball's chance in hell, he produced another paper with all the answers. But they were still in Spanish. I would have to learn every question and every answer, off by heart.

'It's impossible!' I said.

'Take it home with you, and take all the time you need,' he said. 'You'll see, it will work.'

'I'd need at least two years!' I said hopelessly.

'There is no other way,' he said, shrugging his shoulders.

I went home bowed with disappointment and worry. I had thought I would have a few selected questions to deal with, and now I had one hundred, and in a language which I had far from mastered. But there was nothing for it. I chased the children from the room and began. How I crammed! My wife would creep up with fortifying cups of coffee while I sweated. I learned every question, its number and answer, until I could either write them down or answer them orally. I insisted we go to Tegucigalpa at once. But there was still more to learn: suitable lines for the introductory conversation with the examiner.

'He will greet you with *"Buenos dias, Capitan!"*,' the lawyer said, 'And *"Como esta Usted?"*, and you must reply *"Bien gracias y Usted?"* He will then ask "And you intend to become a Honduran citizen?" (all in Spanish, of course), to which you must reply, "I shall be a good Honduran citizen, senor".'

On alighting at the Foreign Department in Tegucigalpa, I must have appeared quite cross-eyed and bemused. It was time to raise the curtain on the whole comedy.

The whole scene went rather more easily than I expected. As luck would have it, the Chief Examiner was partially deaf, and my lawyer was able to cover up a bit and round off my vague answers with some sort of coherence, distracting the man when all else failed. The answers tumbled out and I began to feel cautiously optimistic. Then he took out the bag from which he would randomly draw the questions on which everything now hung. My fate was in the balance. Somehow, I produced an answer for every question, but the last was also the longest and most difficult. The Examiner seemed to appreciate this, and waxed merciful. He wrote down another number. I continued with pen and paper to write my answers, beads of sweat forming on my forehead. Whenever I thought an answer was doubtful, I would smudge the vital word with a blot of ink. At last I was finished, and passed the paper over for him to scrutinize.

There really are times in a man's life when time stands still, or even appears to go backwards. Those next minutes were the most agonizing I shall ever experience in this life. Despair and triumph balanced on a knife-edge. At last the Examiner put the paper slowly down on the table, allowed his face the suggestion of a smile, rose and offered me his hand in a congratulatory handshake. My head reeled. I rose on rubber legs and gave him my hand.

The Examiner broke into a babble of Spanish with the lawyer, then came over and patted me on the back. I wiped the sweat from my brow, and offered him a cigarette with a friendly smile, lighting one for myself. So the formalities came to an end.

I signed a few papers, got a kind of confirmation, and took my leave with a polished '*Hasta luego, senor!*' ('See you later' — but I was really thinking: I hope it will be a long time before we meet again!

As we left, the lawyer said, 'I think we've made it!' And, sure enough, the paper was accepted. I sat in the car in a state of collapse, peace and relief slowly seeping through me. Things were much simpler at the next office — some new papers and a new register to sign, and more questions about the son of the mining engineer who had come to Honduras in the thirties. After all that, we could go and have a well-earned whisky and soda. I enjoyed a cordial evening with friends of the lawyer, and the next day, back in Panama, I was able to pay him the second instalment of his fee. Now I could begin to think of my plans for Norway.

How I had managed everything I shall never know. Every time I think back to the obstacles which faced me then, I break out in a cold sweat. But I had my back to the wall. The change from simple son of a mining engineer to qualified Sea Captain was no easy metamorphosis, and it was a very relieved citizen who returned to Panama at the end of it all. My passport was my most precious treasure.

And so to New York with a United States visa in my brand new passport. At a stopover in Jamaica free Rum-Collins, and I bought souvenirs like any other tourist. A few days sightseeing in New York in the company of my sister and her friends, and lunch with executives of the Chartering Corporation greatly added to my stock of knowledge of how they get things done over there. On the flight to Oslo we stopped over at Gander and there I saw a familiar figure leaving the plane — none other than HRH the Crown Prince, later HM King Olav V of Norway, himself. He was received at Gardemoen with full honours, and later the same day I saw the three Scandinavian monarchs, Haakon, Gustav and Fredrik, side by side in a fine procession through the streets.

The Honduran Consul, whose assistance had been so futile at the outset, now made an equally futile demand for Kr 20,000 — which I settled with Kr 150! Through my lawyer, I informed the Registrar of shipping that the ship was one hundred per cent mine and that I was now a Honduran citizen. A certain minister, Evensen, said: 'We shall try, by any means at our disposal, to prohibit Wilson from taking that ship out of Norwegian registry.' The ship was at that time loading timber in Finland, bound for Egypt.

Naturally I was furious. I told my lawyer I would go straight to Finland, take over the ship, and change her registry to Panama. In this the lawyer restrained me, saying he would handle the whole matter and advising me to return to Panama and wait. After finishing discharging at Alexandria, I took the ship to the USA and still ran her under the Norwegian flag — with full benefits and not a cent to pay in taxes.

Most of the time I was on board with Captain Eilertsen as Master, in the sugar trade from Cuba. One day we came to discharge in Philadelphia and the Norwegian Consul warned Captain Eilertsen that he was sailing under false colours. He was not permitted to sail under the Norwegian flag, the ship was no longer Norwegian, and his licence could be in danger. Whereupon I immediately arranged for Panamanian papers and registry.

We got the Norwegian and Panamanian Consuls on board and ceremoniously lowered the Norwegian flag and raised the Panamanian one. Most of the crew, including the Master, then signed off; they did not want to sail under a foreign flag.

(Soon afterwards, during a short visit to Norway, my grand old lawyer related the hilarious outcome of this escapade. After lengthy deliberation, the powers peevishly decided to close the loophole which I had discovered in the law. A 'Lex Wilson' was added. They had to accept that I had fooled them to the top of their bent. The ship was declared clear to leave Norwegian Registry.)

5

Sailing Under New Colours

Now Captain of my own ship, I found a new crew and sailed for New York to pick up a general cargo for Guatemala and Honduras. There would be no tugs or pilots available in these two small harbours of the Caribbean, and precious little of anything else in the way of facilities. Upon arrival, I sent my Chief Officer forward and the Second Officer aft with the Bosun. Feeling utterly alone on the bridge, I manoeuvred the ship up to the jetty. I let go anchor a little off, to facilitate getting out again, and put her alongside as gently as a maiden's kiss. The performance went perfectly, and was repeated at the second harbour, except that, when we left, I went the wrong side of a mark and nearly grounded her. We crept ahead at a snail's pace with everyone holding their breath. There could not have been more than an inch of water beneath the keel. To the surprise of all, myself included, the operation went beautifully.

That little piece of luck was the last we had for quite a while — the freight market went into a slump and we had to anchor up right there in Central America and phone New York every day, hoping for news.

'Can't you get us *something?*'

'We're working on it, but there is nothing yet. Ring again tomorrow.'

After about three weeks, word came through that we had got a cargo of sugar from Cuba for Mobile, Alabama. We sailed for Cuba in ballast and loaded the sugar, but, after discharging at Mobile, we were again without any cargo. I was optimistic, as all beginners are. Something would turn up. Meanwhile, I put the ship into a shipyard for its four-yearly special survey.

Though the cost was reasonable, I ran up a bill there and with the local ship-suppliers. Just as all was ready, we got news of another sugar cargo from Cuba. I went happily up the shipyard office with the news.

'We're sailing tomorrow,' I said. 'We have a cargo of sugar to collect from Cuba.'

'Fine,' they said, 'but what about the bills?'

'Oh, they will be paid,' I replied, green as ever and thinking in European terms. 'We'll remit on our return to the States.'

'No.' They shook their heads. 'You won't do that. You don't leave this port until your bills are paid.'

Half an hour later a Sheriff came on board, complete with ten gallon hat and six shooter. He attached a placard to the mast which read: SHIP ARRESTED, and went on to seal up my cabin.

And there she stayed for three months.

The market was at rock bottom, and there was no hope of finding a cargo. I decided to try my luck in New York and left the ship in the care of the Chief Officer and the Bosun, both Norwegians. I rented a little room in a cheap hotel off Times Square, where I paid $3 a day, shared a shower and did my laundry in a small tub out at the back. Time seemed to stand still.

This was the tightest corner I had ever found myself in. I was advised by my New York agents to approach a well-to-do Norwegian shipowner called Torrey Mosvold. I travelled out to his sprawling Manhattan estate, which he told me had been acquired from a banker's widow. I should mention that the said banker committed suicide in the thirties and left his wife without support. It was an unpleasant experience: humiliating and wearying to an appalling degree. I was offered apples from the garden by way of refreshment and in the end it was agreed that he would help me by taking ownership of the vessel and offering me a position as Master for very low wages. I arrived back in my $3 room in a state of utter dejection. Frozen to the marrow, I slept for some ten hours.

My 'Saviour' had his inspector aboard my ship the very next day, but now I refused his kind offer. Even dire misfortune must have an end, after all, and that incident was indeed the rock bottom of my career as a shipowner. Soon afterwards I was put in touch with another buyer who came over from Finland, and we travelled together to view the ship. I took great care to keep him plied with drinks, of which he imbibed a great quantity, as we were *en route*.

He liked the *Penelope*, and everything seemed to be in order. But then we learned that currency restrictions had been applied and that the bank would not release the money from Finland. He would return home. Now both thoroughly inebriated, we decided to return to New York to see what could be done. Presenting ourselves next day at the office of my agents, the Finnish captain told them that he planned to return home.

'You can't do that, Captain,' they told him. 'The arrangements have now progressed so far that you would not be permitted to leave.' I knew this to be bluff. The Captain did not argue, but took his leave and returned to his hotel.

'You shouldn't have said that,' I told the agent. 'He knows very well that you cannot stop him.' I could see the whole deal falling through. I left in a hurry and button-holed the Captain in his room.

'Captain,' I said, 'Let's have a talk.'

He was unenthusiastic.

'You know,' he told me, 'I was sitting there with the ticket in my pocket. I am leaving today. I knew your agent could do nothing, but I did not care to talk to him.'

'I knew so too,' I said, 'and it was an extremely silly thing to do. But now, Captain, *I* have a proposal for you. If you can somehow turn this deal, I will give you £5,000.' That was a large percentage of the ship's price, which was in any case at rock bottom. 'Money in your pocket,' I continued, 'and no need for a receipt.'

That got a warmer reception. 'Well,' he said, 'that proposal I like, and I will see if I can swing it. It is a very nice amount of money for me, and of course it is between us two only.'

Very soon he had the matter satisfactorily concluded and I instructed the agents to pay him the £5,000. I had previously contacted my wife and warned her that we might have to live in Finland for a while on 'frozen Finnish pounds'; she should stand by. But as it turned out, that was not necessary, and another plan materialized.

I now chartered the ship back from the Finnish captain, who was also part owner, for six months. The market began to pick up again and we got good freight rates. The first cargo was sugar

from Havana, and it was while loading there that I felt the need
for a break. The worry and strain of the last months and the
completion of the negotiations for the sale of the *Penelope* had
left me in a state of nerves and somewhat drained. I suggested
to the Chief Officer that we take a day off and go to the beach
and generally unwind.

We went ashore to an idyllic shaded beach restaurant and
began with a few drinks. It was not long before some girls turned
up and a band began to serenade our table. The afternoon wore
on and our spirits rose as the sun sank. It would be an
understatement to say we were inebriated. To this day I cannot
recall how I got aboard the plane. Perhaps I was carried on. I
only remember collapsing in the toilets in the plane and being
revived by a couple of other passengers, who by dint of massage
and copious libations of cold water, managed to get me on my
feet and back to my seat.

I emerged from the plane at Panama in a very sorry state,
hair dishevelled and white suit crumpled and dirty, to be met
by my wife and new-born son. My poor wife burst into tears. I
suggested we go home and celebrate with a few drinks, but wiser
friends steered me into bed instead. The next day I brought her
up to date on the trying time I had had, and she realized I had
suffered some sort of breakdown. I had told the Chief Officer I
would rest at home in Panama during the charter period, and
that is in fact what happened.

In May 1949, having re-delivered the ship to the owners in
New York, I signed on as a supernumerary, and we sailed up
to Newfoundland. The Finnish captain was markedly cool
towards me during this voyage. He had picked up a cargo of
timber for Liverpool, and his lack of enthusiasm persisted right
until we arrived there and I signed off. I did not learn the reason
for his behaviour until twenty years had passed. I attended the
Cape Horner Congress in Oslo in 1969, with the barquentine
Regina Maris, and met him among the guests. I invited him
aboard for a drink. He was not particularly eager, but in the
end his curiosity got the better of him: 'It could be interesting
to see what the last Cape Horner looked like'. Over a glass in
my salon I at last heard the reason for his coolness: he had never
received the £5,000 I had promised him — only a token sum.
I was flabbergasted to hear he had been cheated out of it by the
New York agent, and that this had gnawed at him all these

years. His bitterness evaporated with the drink, however, and we ended up good friends once more.

From Liverpool I made my way to London. I had arranged to meet my brother Sigfried and go to the Isle of Wight to look at a large sea-going tug which was up for sale. I had seen the possibility of doing business salvaging tuna-fishing vessels (which frequently broke down) out of Panama. The tub appeared satisfactory in every respect, but I began to doubt if I really knew enough about tug work. I decided to make my way back to New York. I got myself a free passage on board a Swedish ship, and the first evening aboard, before we sailed, turned out to be one big round of heavy drinking. The next morning, the captain invited me to his quarters for some more beer and aquavit, and informed me that I could not travel with them after all because of insurance technicalities. Somehow (I am hazy as to details), I reached London and got them to hold me the last seat on a New York bound Stratocruiser, as those two-deck planes were then called. I recall the rush out to the airport as the plane stood cleared for take-off, and dimly remember sitting next to an Egyptian lady who lived in France and was travelling to New York on a shopping spree.

The best advice I got in New York was to return to Panama and wait while they tried to find a ship for me. In a very tired state I made my way back to my wife and family and waited a few days. On being recalled to New York I learned that they had found a ship which might suit me. This was the twenty-six year old *Nortuna*, owned by Erling Naess and laid up in Bremen in Germany. The price was $95,000. I went over to see her, and rusty and old as she was in appearance, she looked to me like the stuff of dreams. I put down $50,000, and Naess was to continue in ownership until I had paid off the difference, which took me three years. In 1958, after running her for nine years, I sent her with a cargo of coal to Japan and sold her there for scrap, thus obtaining the freight and scrap values combined.

Some time after the purchase of the *Nortuna*, I heard from my brother in Norway about a visit he had had from the tax department. In their wisdom they had seen fit to present us with a demand for some NKr 1,950,000. Household effects and personal belongings would be assessed and appropriated in default of payment, if necessary. Sigfried, completely taken aback, showed them reverently into his room. Spartan was hardly the word for it. The sole furniture consisted of a rickety table topped with an ancient and honourable 1920's Underwood typewriter, and a chair to match. It was now the turn of the taxman to be speechless. In a state of apoplexy he backed slowly from the room and, as in all the best adventure stories, was never seen again. A good thing, too, or I would have been ruined!

After settling with Erling Naess, I proceeded to make the *Nortuna* ready for sea. I found an excellent crew and signed on three German Master Mariners as my First, Second and Third Officers, and three Chief Engineers, two of them as Second and Third Engineer. I also found good engine assistants and deck crew. Thanks to these fine seamen and engineers, we were able to get the ship over to Panama and down to Chile to load for Mobile, Alabama.

I soon discovered that the overall condition of the ship was deplorable. When we raised steam we found leaking boiler tubes in two of the boilers, which had to be plugged. In the meantime we put steam on deck for the sixteen winches. The pipes leaked everywhere and all the winches were worn down and out of order. My new engine team set to work with a will and together with the shipyard brought some kind of order out of the mess. It was just after the war and everyone was extremely happy to have this opportunity to go back to work. It was this that was indeed the salvation of the whole venture. Reasonable wages and costs, no taxes and a reduced crew made the difference between feast and famine.

Unbelievable luck attended us from the start. I should first have taken a cargo over to the States and then sailed in ballast to Panama to deliver the ship to the charterers, but this was cancelled and it was thought better to sail direct to Panama in ballast. In the meantime I had already taken on fuel for a longer voyage. We duly arrived in Panama, where the ship was inspected by the charterers, and were then ordered to go to the fuel pier for bunkers. But the Chief Engineer informed me that there was *no more fuel* — not even enough to start our engines! We therefore had to be taken by tug to the fuel oil pier. The 'fuel oil' which I already had on board was 300 tons of solidified sludge. Not even the most powerful American suction pumps could removed it, and we had to put men at it with shovels and spades. The work took ten days.

Bunkering finally completed, we proceeded to Tocopilla, Chile, to load nitrate for Mobile. One or two of the boilers gave us constant trouble and had to be cooled down so that we could plug leaking tubes. However, we got safely to Tocopilla, and here I sold the grain, shifting boards used on the last voyage by Erling Naess, and realized a tidy sum. My boiler difficulties continued, and I had to bribe the stevedores to hide the fact that there was not enough steam to drive the winches and that the ship was out of trim at departure time. *En route* to the Panama Canal we had to use all our available water just to keep the boilers going. On arrival we had even run out of drinking water. All this could have landed us with enormous expenses by way of claims. The ship was trimmed by the head, which is, of course, prohibited; she had a three degree list; and to top it all, we were eighteen inches overloaded, in spite of the fact that we had not a drop of boiler water left and were taking more fuel oil in Cristobal! On sailing from Cristobal there was nothing to be seen of the Plimsoll lines, but the list and trim had been corrected by the fresh-water tanks. That not a single claim was made, nor orders given for us to be tugged right through the canal, nor any attempt made to detain us until the ship was seaworthy, I think deserves a place in the Guiness Book of Records.

In Mobile, I decided that something had to be done. We would change all the boiler tubes — some 1100 of them — overhaul all the fuel pumps and renew the fuel oil injectors. The latter were of diverse types and were to be replaced by one brand. Several other modifications and repairs were necessary before the ship could be left for the Chief Engineer to take her back to Chile to load for Alexandria, Egypt. We would have all the sludge dug out of the tanks, some 300 tons, which twice had very nearly caused the catastrophe of being adrift at sea — which would have meant salvage and probably the end of my career.

When the discharging of the cargo was finished and the harbour pilot on board, I asked for steam to the anchor windlass. The Chief Engineer then told me (again!) that we had no more fuel oil. I had steam delivered from a tug, and when the anchor was up we were towed down to the shipyard — 'Dead Ship'.

I must here relate the story of the result of my asking for a price for changing the 1100 boiler tubes. Three different shipyards tendered their prices, and the one I accepted was $18,000. The next bid was $24,000, and then came the surprise — a smiling pleasant gentleman from the third shipyard came on board to me with his price — $34,000 . . . 'But' — he told me — 'Captain, I have included $10,000 — for your pocket.'

I consoled him and offered him a drink as I told him I was also the owner of the ship and would of course take the lowest price. I was really afraid that he was about to faint.

By the time we left Cristobal, bound for Egypt, we were about a foot below the marks, but over the years it was often more than that. I have calculated that in overloaded cargoes alone I must have taken 27,000 tons per ship during the charter period of seven years. In Curaçao I took on more fuel-oil for the round trip to Europe, thus reducing the cost of refuelling in Europe, where the prices were considerably higher.

On arrival in the Mediterranean I decided to call in at Gibraltar. I had had some problems with the crew and decided to put ashore three firemen and a deck-hand who were trouble makers. It was my first encounter with British officialdom, and their manner struck me as distinctly unaccommodating.

'You can't do this, Captain,' they said.

'Why not?' I queried. 'They have broken their contracts, and, in accordance with my rights as Master, I am putting them ashore for repatriation under sea law.'

'But it's almost Christmas,' one of them insisted. 'They ought at least to have some extra money for celebrating.'

I thought that a daft argument, but they could have made things extremely difficult for me: it would be ruinous financially and disastrous personally if my licence were to be put in jeopardy. I understood I would not be allowed to sail until I had agreed to their demands. I added a few pounds to my commission from the ship-chandler and left them with that. I had got off lightly.

Two days out of Gibraltar one of the engineer assistants badly damaged his hand. I had to land him in Oran, Algeria, for hospital treatment. We went on to discharge in Alexandria and left in ballast.

In order to avoid using the double-bottom tanks both for ballast and fuel-oil, which fosters the production of sludge and creates problems for the engineers, we tried filling holds four and five with water, where the tunnel shaft would have the same stabilizing effect as the grain shifting boards. After lowering the hatch beams to hold down the wooden sealing on the tank tops, we filled in water. Unfortunately, the beams proved to be too light for this purpose and we had to pump the water out again and fill the double-bottom tanks with ballast. It was arduous work to replace the ceiling afterwards.

We now ran into very bad weather. A series of continuous storms up to hurricane force met us and we had to take shelter in the lee of islands and various points of land for several nights. Winter in the Mediterranean can be atrocious, and to add to our difficulties we had dysentery on board, putting six men in bed and leaving us with very little in the way of medicaments.

I radioed Oran to send us the necessary medicines with our engineer assistant. The weather eased up and we anchored in the roads outside Oran. To my horror, there now approached a boat laden with officials: customs, police, immigration authorities, etc. Our engineer assistant came aboard minus three fingers but otherwise in good form. I turned on the officials.

'What are you doing here and where are the medicines?' I asked in considerable anger.

'We must first clear you in and deal with all the formalities . . .'

'Oh, no, you don't,' I cut them short. 'I am not going into your bloody port, and you get yourselves back into that boat before I have my crew throw you in the water.' I was unshaven and worn down with nights of riding the storms.

'You can't do that, Captain,' they protested feebly.

'Yes I can, and I *will!*' I was ready for anything.

'OK. We will report you to the Consul.' I suppose they thought the ship was Norwegian. They retreated down the gangway.

I now got under way across the Atlantic without any medicines, and had to remove the stitches from the hand of the engineer and dress the wound as best I could. Half a day out and another storm blew up, and we had to seek shelter anew. In easier weather we sailed once more, and had just reached the shelter of some islands off Cape Bon when yet another storm loomed. It took twice as long as usual to get from Alexandria to the Straits of Gibraltar and I was concerned to find an explanation to give the charterers. The ship had suffered in the bad weather and the Chief Engineer pointed out that the propeller shaft was badly out of alignment.

I was at a loss to know what to do, until a bright idea again struck me: an *Average Repoort*, of course! Into the log from both the Chief Engineer and myself.

And so it was we rolled across the Atlantic and reached Curaçao, where we refuelled, thence through the Canal and down to Tocopilla for another load of nitrate for Philadelphia. Here the ship was dry-docked at the same yard from which she had been launched in 1920: Sun Shipbuilding Company. We were there for a month, during which time the propeller shaft was re-aligned and some of the storm damage repaired. The bill for the shaft alone came to $40,000, and when the main engine and auxiliaries had been overhauled the total stood at $300,000! All this on top of $60,000 bill we had run up in Mobile on the previous trip. Eighty per cent of the costs were met by the underwriters, but some of the insurance company's executives came near to losing their jobs, and my insurance statistics suffered badly.

Our ship was now in good order. Our main trade was nitrate to the USA or Europe, and for a long time we were employed bringing return cargoes of coal to an iron foundry in the south of Chile. This was not an easy combination because the ship had to be meticulously cleaned after a cargo of coal. As she had two 'tween decks, it was a prodigious task, carried out during the ballast journey from southern to northern Chile. Everyone on board had to help in this work, and I was alone on the bridge, steering the ship from morning till night. Another miracle of cleaning was also needed before we could take on a sugar cargo after a coal one, or even a nitrate one.

6

The Influence Of Alcohol

The Influence of Alcohol might not seem the best phrase with which
to launch a section on the financing of a shipping company, but
I am stuck with it, and it is, in any case, very relevant. I might
even call it a subject close to my heart. I get hot under the collar
when people produce figures of deaths attributed to alcohol. I
have yet to see figures showing the number of *births* attributable
to alcohol, which would surely be of more positive interest, since
nobody lives for ever.

Alcohol produces at least two good effects: the loosening of
tongues and the generation of ideas. Our charterers in Santiago
also had an office in New York and one in London — an
endearing bunch whom I christened the Pickwick Club. It was
over drinks with Oscar at the Santiago office that I got wind of
something: the charterers were interested in obtaining a couple
of ideal ships for their nitrate trade. I immediately began to get
some sound ideas. I pressed him further, but he realized his
lapse and tried to cover it up.

'Just forget it, John,' he said.

But I was agog. 'It sounds very interesting to me, Oscar,' I
said. 'Let's talk about it tomorrow. I am sure I can be of
assistance.'

'No, John,' he insisted, 'it's really nothing. Think no more of
it.'

In the morning, with somewhat less of a hangover than
Oscar, I again broached the subject.

'I am on my way to New York and can raise the matter with
Hinton there. I am absolutely sure in my own mind that we can
work out something concrete on the lines.'

Oscar began to show a little more interest, and the result was that I was soon afterwards presenting myself in the New York office with a blueprint of the vessels, based on my experience in the trade over a number of years. I knew exactly what a ship carrying alternate loads of nitrate, sugar and coal should be like, down to the last detail.

With unwavering enthusiasm I pressed my plans on them until I at last felt I was beginning to make some impression. They agreed to meet me again in Santiago the next time I was in Chile for loading, and they would go into the matter in more detail. At this meeting we produced draft proposals specifying details and particulars for the construction of two prototype ships for the Chilean nitrate trade, and these were laid before the charterers.

For the financing, we would have to have a seven year charter on which we could raise the money and have the ships built. This would be in Japan, where I had already done some groundwork and acquired the necessary information on costs, which were very reasonable because of certain subsidies in operation at the time, a privilege which marked a decided advantage.

Although high finance is not my strong point, I had the satisfaction of seeing my proposals accepted by the Nitrate Corporation and I was soon in Japan getting down to more detailed discussions on costs and dates with the shipbuilders.

Cleaning the coal out of all the nooks and crannies and angles and pockets of an old ship is a painstaking task, and I gave much thought to how it could be made easier. The result was that I came up with suggested modification to the builders of my two new ships which did away with all of the angles and pockets employed in the construction. Where possible, all angles were slanted so that we could wash each hold down quickly and effectively with hoses. This would reduce the work of cleaning from days to hours. The charterers accepted all my suggestions, even to the point of substituting cranes for winches. This was to the benefit of both the charterers and myself.

Conventional ships carrying nitrate on one trip and sugar or coal on the next certainly had problems. Six electric cranes with easily removable motors were installed in such a way that I could use two for any one hold, or had one spare crane in case of breakdown. Water hoses with valves were installed in all holds, thus avoiding the necessity of transporting equipment between holds. The old-fashioned and expensive shifting boards used for carrying grain were replaced with a rigid system erected by the crew. This was accepted by the USCG and worked perfectly for all the years I used it. I also suggested the installation of McGregor hatch covers, which are in universal use today. My ideas appeared radical at the time, but were all incorporated in the specifications for the two vessels — though I was reminded that it was all at my own risk!

The work of those years was a considerable strain, and I would go far to lighten the lot of my crew. It was hard for them to find work, and I had a good bunch of men, mostly Panamanians and Chileans. They signed on for very modest wages — subsistence at times was as little as sixty-five cents a day, compared with some eight or ten dollars as I write. I had, of course, no steward, only a cook and galleyboy, and had to order provisions myself. In order to reduce the cost of beef, I bought domestic cattle in southern Chile during discharging. I would go to auction in the early morning and buy seven oxen each time, arranging for a boy to walk them down to the slaughterhouse. I would pay the butcher by leaving him the hides and intestines, and would then rent a truck and drive the beef to the ship.

I well remember one particular occasion. The farmer had mistimed matters in giving one of the animals a lot of salt a little too early, with the result that just before climbing on the scales it urinated all the water which it needed to make the weight up. How I laughed when in an ecstasy of rage he slapped the animal on the rump.

The slaughtering was an inhuman and nerve-racking affair. Rather than using a slaughter mask to knock the animal out, they jerked a small knife into the neck, thereby paralysing the creature. They would then slash the throat and leave the animal to bleed to death. I have seen some animals rise to their feet again before collapsing — a very distressing sight.

On one occasion I bought some twenty tons of deep-frozen surplus wartime beef — it was not the very best quality, but then I paid next to nothing for it.

I am tempted to recall here an episode which, although amusing, could easily have resulted in tragedy. Swordfish are to be found in abundance off the coast of Chile, and I invited the Port Captain of Tocopilla for a day's sport harpooning them with my gun. We planned to go out on a Sunday. I warned the Chief Engineer and asked him to prepare the ship's motor lifeboat. On the Wednesday he came to me with the news that the motor needed a major overhaul and could not possibly be ready by Sunday. I knew we would be in port for more than two weeks, so, at the Port Captain's suggestion, we postponed the trip to the following Sunday. Early the following week I went to inspect the boat and see how the work was progressing. I stepped on board and my foot went straight through the bottom. The engineer told me he was waiting for parts from America.

'We'll have to look into this here, as well,' I said, showing him the foot-sized hole in the bottom.

We got the engineers to patch up the hole, together with many others that they found while they were at it. We then checked the other three boats, and found twenty holes in the first two, while the third had no bottom at all. What rivets we had were soon used up on the first three, but the last called for more drastic action. On a bottom made of canvas and wire netting we laid a thin covering of cement which, when dry, we continued to build up until all was satisfactory. When we came to check the watertight air tanks, they were also found to be full of holes. We resorted to a glue-like compound we found on board, unshipped the tanks, coated them and reinstalled them in the boats.

The fire and lifeboat drills incumbent on a present day shipmaster were beyond us in those days, faced as we were with constant financial problems and the necessity of driving the ship to the utmost. I needed the crew all the time for the repair and upkeep of the ship, and we could never afford the luxury of such drills, except once. It was a Sunday, I remember and some whim made me suggest we try out our 'cement' boat. We were, after all, relatively up to date for once with our work, and could afford to indulge ourselves a little. In any case, if we ever needed a boat, that one seemed the best bet. But it was no sooner launched than it went straight to the bottom, lingering only just long enough for us to get a *lanchero* to spike the watertight air cases in case they would keep the wreck afloat. And that was the end of our cement boat and our one and only lifeboat drill. Our fire hoses were, of course, absolutely rotten, and could never have been used in drill or in danger.

Though we never had a fire drill, we did once have a tragic

fire on board. We were alongside at St Vincente. I was down in Number Five Hold with an American Bureau surveyor when we saw a flame coming down from the deck above. I shouted to him to rush up to the deck, but, being heavier and slower than I, he took rather longer to escape than I did, and his back was badly burned. I received a slight burn on the back of my neck. The fire brigade came aboard at once, and the firemen stood around in their fine uniforms with their modern oxygen equipment, not venturing to go down into the smoking hold because of the poor visibility. I knew my way around in the hold and beseeched them to lend me their equipment, as I knew there were still men down there, but they would not agree. I grabbed a rope, took a deep breath and rushed down the ladder. I found a man lying at the foot of the ladder, fastened the rope around him and had him hauled to safety. Then I went down again, and managed to find another three men. Sadly, the last was already dead. The Mayor of the town gave me an award for this feat of rescue.

The cause of it all was that I had wanted to remove most of the lower 'tween decks in order to facilitate the loading of bulk cargoes and avoid trimming there. In Number Four Hold part of the 'tween deck was the tank top of an 800-ton fuel oil tank which, although empty as we were burning away the deck-plating, was not, of course, free of gas. We barely avoided a very serious explosion when I caught one of the men as he was about to turn his burning equipment on the tank top plating, thinking it was deck-plate. The fire itself started because the oxygen cylinders for the burning equipment had been left in the lower 'tween decks (quite against regulations, of course), and the cock on one of them was either leaking or inadequately closed. Moreover, the gas hoses were not long enough to permit the cylinders to be brought up on deck without extra — and to the workman, unnecessary — effort.

Another tragic accident occurred while deck-plates were being hoisted by crane. Some plates had been slung together in a slipshod manner, and during hoisting one part slipped out and fell on a workmen, killing him instantly. The workmen were afraid to go down in the hold for three days after that for fear of the dead man's ghost. And whispers were heard in various brothels around Tocopilla that we would never reach our destination in the USA!

During the voyage to Mobile, we sprung a leak in Number Four Hold. It was well below the water line, where a plate had simply rusted right through and water was coming in behind a frame. We tried everything we could think of to stop the leak, but the pressure was too great, and the leak itself soon became inaccessible. A leak-mat strapped outside did nothing to help, and the water continued to rise, despite the unrelenting efforts of all the men struggling in the water and nitrate in the hold. Eventually there was so much water in the hold that we could no longer enter, and we gave up the unequal struggle and closed the hatch.

The water soon began to seep into the bilges, and this we tackled with the bilge pumps. However, the combination of water and nitrate was too much for the pumps to handle, and they were soon worn out. We were now off the western point of Cuba, and the ship was virtually wallowing in the water. To make matters worse, we got warning of a hurricane approaching. I called a ship's council with the ship's officers and representatives from the crew, and discussed the options open to us. We could call in at Cuba, but I was dubious as to what kind of assistance could be got there. Or we could continue for Mobile, since most hurricanes usually swung north-east and we should be clear. That was what I recommended, and this was unanimously approved.

We swung out all four lifeboats, ready for launching at a moment's notice, and everybody packed a small bag containing their papers and valuables. Two of my children were with me on that trip, during their school holidays (several years before my first wife had left for Norway with our baby son, while I had the two girls in a boarding school in Panama). The hurricane followed us through the shark-infested water all the way into the Gulf of Mexico. Once off Mobile, we picked up the pilot and I told him our story, instructing him to put us right on the nearest sandbank or we would sink. This he did in the nick of time, and we called out the fire department with their pumps and equipment. I cabled our port engineer, who came down at once from New York, and ordered tugs to take us to the discharging wharf as soon as the flooded hold had been pumped dry.

The other holds were discharged normally, but the nitrate in Number Four Hold was so hard it had to be dug out when the ship was in dry dock. The leaking plate was replaced and the hold cleaned out and painted, all at the underwriter's expense. I should note that one of those lifeboats which we had swung ready during that perilous voyage was the one in which we had invited the Port Captain of Tocopilla to take a tour. We finally got the motor spares after a wait of two years!

The Panama Canal grew to be major headache for a shipmaster with overloading or trim problems. Their limits were always more exacting, and, should the ship have even as little as half a degree of list, they would call out the tugs, the cost of which would run to some $1,000. Alternatively, we would be refused transit. Looking back on it, I wonder how, during those days, I was ever allowed through. My ship was always loaded to the marks, but with no water on board. We filled water in the canal, and more fuel oil after the transit. All those years we almost never had any other drinking water than what we got from the canal, thus saving ourselves another expense.

In this connection I could also mention another occasion when, although already overloaded, I took on enough fuel in Curaçao for the round trip to Europe. That resulted in a big saving for the charterers, who had instructed me to refuel in Europe, but of course it put the ship even deeper into the water, as we were now *very* overloaded!

I had two German officers aboard at the time who had ingratiated themselves into the company of my brother and his wife. They were, in fact, very friendly, and the four were frequently to be seen together in bars and restaurants ashore. Just before we sailed from Curaao, the two Germans went to the pilot office and informed them that we were overloaded and that the matter should be 'looked into'. I learned of this and the ruin loomed. I sat brooding in my office, awaiting the arrival of the pilot. Would he order part of the cargo off-loaded, with consequent delays and extra costs for re-shipping, hiring etc., etc? It was simply too awful to contemplate. Once again my fate seemed to be hanging in the balance. I would know as soon as the door opened. The pilot's footsteps approached along the deck . . . There was a slight pause before he knocked at the door.

'Come in,' I heard myself saying.

'Good morning, Captain,' he said. Non-committal, I thought.

'Good morning, Mr Pilot,' I answered, staring at him with an air of resignation.

'Your Second and Third Officers, what kind of men are they?'

'Well,' I faltered, 'they are German . . . ' I was at a loss.

'They have been up in my office with some story,' he went on, declining my offer of a seat. I offered him a cigarette and a light. He inhaled deeply, a reflective look on his face, and passed the blue smoke out through closed teeth like one making an important decision.

'All right, Captain,' he said, 'let's go along to the bridge and get under way.'

I was taken completely by surprise. We let go fore and aft, and off we went. When it came to the point of putting him ashore again, I was uncertain what line to take. Cigarettes and drink are duty free in the Island. Then I remembered that his jacket was still hanging in my office. I slipped away and put $100 in the pocket.

'Thank you very much, Mr Pilot,' I called, passing him his jacket, which was the light weight type in general use in the tropics.

'No trouble at all, Captain,' were his parting words.

I was dazed with relief, and have since thought much about this episode. Did his deft fingers learn so much in the moment he accepted the jacket? I will never know. I never saw him again.

We now set sail for Italy to discharge our cargo and for me to marry for the second time. My fiancée and her mother and brother were to meet me at La Spezia. Her father was my Chief Officer. I had met his daughter during a short visit to his home. I had asked my lawyer in Panama to put the divorce from my first wife in order. I had also made preparations for the forthcoming wedding without having the papers at hand — so I began to wonder whether I was about to commit bigamy. However, two days after arriving in Italy, the papers came in the mail, whereupon we travelled to Genoa and were married at the Panamanian Consulate. I took three weeks off for a honeymoon, leaving the ship in the care of my brother Sigfried. We visited Rome, Capri, the Blue Grotto and all the many sights which, though considered commonplace today, were then the prerogative of the so-called jet set. I had put my two German trouble-makers ashore, and thought I might contact the Mafia with a view to dealing them the retribution they so richly deserved — but nothing came of it.

Running these old ships was not just a question of keeping them in circulation, but also of coming through, or avoiding if at all possible, the numerous checks and surveys which waylaid one in the process of trying to maintain the ever-tightening schedules. The only way to do this was with a little healthy bribery.

I remember being due for our four yearly special survey in Chile. As luck would have it, our surveyor bore a fine sounding English name — that always looked convincing on a report. He was, in fact, a Chilean, and could speak very little English. His task was to check the double-bottom tanks and put them under pressure; after that they would be emptied and the manholes opened to allow them to be inspected from within. While the tanks were supposedly being filled, the surveyor and I sat drinking whisky and soda. When we were informed that the tanks were now under full pressure, we went down to inspect them for leaks and damage. In fact, there was not a drop of water in them, so of course there were no leaks to be seen. Seeing that everything was in order, we went back to my salon for more whisky while the tanks were pumped out and the covers removed for internal inspection. That took about two hours, after which I told the surveyor that he could go down and check the insides. I hastened to explain that the tanks were rather dirty on account of their being used partly for fuel oil and partly for ballast water, and that we would have to fit him out with special clothing so that he would not get unduly dirty.

We now dressed him up in oil skins, boots and gloves, until he was practically immobilized, and I went quickly down ahead of him. I found that one of the manhole covers had been placed bottom up, and was obviously as dry as a bone. I quickly turned it over before he arrived on the scene. He peered down into the dirty tank with a flashlight in his hand, obviously unwilling to go down. He checked out some, but not all, of the remaining tanks in the same way, and seemed satisfied with their condition.

After a return to my salon, we came to the inspection of the condenser. This was leaking so badly that the Chief Engineer advised me that repairs would take twenty-four hours before we could go to sea.

'There is only one thing we can do,' I said. 'Come up later and tell us the condenser is under full pressure, but don't put a drop of water in.'

This he did, and we went down to 'inspect' it. We found it absolutely watertight. After a few more fake inspections, interspersed with visits to my salon, the surveyor pronounced himself satisfied with my vessel and signed his report accordingly. We proceeded to sea with the steam going out through the smoke-stack until we were off the coast, where we drifted while carrying out the necessary repairs.

Going to sea in this way may be compared with a steam locomotive, which passes its steam out into the air. Since such a locomotive can refill with water at any convenient station, it does not need to carry a condenser.

On the topic of old ships, I call to mind an occasion in Hamburg when I, all too exceptionally, had some surplus funds, and decided to use them to improve the ship. We would fix up the stern a little, pick off the rust, and have it painted. But as soon as the workmen started on it with their electric hammers, a whole pattern of cracks appeared. I called at once for the work to stop. As luck would have it, there were no surveyors in the immediate vicinity, and I ordered doublers to be welded on and painted. After that I had still more cement boxes moulded inside and behind the frames. So we sailed on rust and cement boxes reinforced with timber struts.

7

Some People . . .

When I mentioned 'harsh realities' earlier, I was thinking mostly of people, and the harshest reality often comes up in relationships with people we are quite close to. The way an individual can react is often disappointingly harsh.

A man comes aboard in Tocopilla, Chile, and asks for a chance to work his passage to America. We are bound for Virginia with a cargo of nitrate, and I am running on a very tight budget. The last thing I am looking for is an extra hand to pay or mouth to feed. But the fellow — a well-built man in his thirties — persists; he pleads and begs for a chance for himself and his wife to leave Chile, and at last I succumb.

It was winter when we arrived in the Caribbean, and we were met with a pretty hard north-east trade wind. Here it can blow at gale force and, being deep loaded, we were soon rolling our scuppers under. I was suddenly aroused from sleep by the chilling cry of 'Man overboard!' and literally sprang to the bridge. By a series of intricate manoeuvres in abominable seas, we turned the ship through 180? and retraced our path, with every available pair of eyes strained to find a speck of life in the pitiless turbulence. After about fifteen minutes the cry went up: 'There he is!' and no sooner had I approached the helpless figure floating with his scalp split wide open than my brother Sigfried was in the water with a line, and within minutes had secured it around the man. Getting the two men aboard again was tricky, to say the least. While waiting for the ship to roll the right way so as to draw them in over the wash-ports, I suddenly saw sharks, two of the largest specimens I have ever seen. Shaken, I rushed to my cabin to get a revolver, but in my state of nerves I could not open the safe, and had to resort to a small pocket revolver which I planned to try to use to frighten off the sharks. My brother's wife shouted, 'Don't!' after me, thinking I intended to shoot the men, rather than let them be eaten by the sharks. But the sharks simply continued to circle round the two men, keeping their distance — perhaps they had just fed. Without further ado I ordered the men hauled in, and fortunately the ship rolled her scuppers under at that precise moment. The deck crew hauled with a will, and suddenly both men were safely on deck.

The seaman had been standing on the Number Four Hatch trying to get some dramatic photos of the waves when he was washed overboard. His injury consisted of a deep clean cut through the scalp from the nose over the top of his head and down to the back of his neck, laying bare a gleaming cranium. We carried him to the salon table, where it needed four or five of my strongest crewmen to hold him down while I administered chloroform. When he passed out at last I proceeded to shave away what hair I could, my brother's wife helping me by holding the two sides of his face up tight towards the white skull, and I started stitching from the bridge of the nose. With our general state of agitation and the ship's motion, I had more than once to recover the needle from the dirty floor. I used plenty of iodine and antibiotics. After putting in nineteen stitches and cleaning up the face, I recognized him to be the man who wanted to work his passage to America.

A few days on a diet of egg yolks and port wine speeded what turned out to be a remarkable recovery. On arrival in port, he was handed over to the nearest hospital. An hour or two later he reappeared on board, needing no further treatment, and with a message that the captain had done 'a perfect job'. After a few days, he took his discharge.

Harsh realities? Well, a little drama, perhaps; but wait . . .

The man proceeded to New York, accompanied by his wife, and what was his first action? He contacted lawyers and sued me, as owner and company, for a million dollars!

What a beautiful animal is a shark! And to think they were so heartlessly denied a morsel of supper by a cruel, unthinking sea-captain! But in the case of another 'operation' I was sadly not so successful.

Helmuth Rudiger is a name I cannot easily forget: a young German seaman, seventeen years of age, at the start of a promising career. We were in ballast and bound for Iquique to pick up a cargo when he fell from the 'tween deck right down to the bottom, striking the shaft tunnel on the way, and sustaining, among other injuries, a broken thigh.

After administering a total anaesthetic, I was able to stretch the large unwilling muscles enough to allow the misshapen bone ends to meet perfectly. I then encased the whole in plaster of Paris and had it weighted over a roller, in the customary way, on his bed in the ship's sick bay. He appeared well enough, took a few puffs from his cigarette, and seemed to be in no pain. But on arrival at Iquique two days later, where an ambulance was already waiting after our emergency call, he died as soon as he was put ashore, as a result of his internal injuries.

One day I was summoned to treat a boy for a boil on his leg. The Chief Officer had been tampering with it for far too long, and quite ineffectually. It was now a serious case of blood poisoning, with the characteristic black line from the boil to a point above the knee. Under local anaesthetic I cut the boil and an incredible quantity of thick, yellow, porridge-like and bloody matter was drained from the wound. I administered antibiotics daily and kept the sore in wet dressings for two weeks until, finally, the black line had cleared. The wound now looked clean and I let it heal up, with the result that leg and life were saved. The boy, an apprentice, was none the worse for his ordeal when he signed off in Castro's Cuba.

I dealt with many other cases, venereal and otherwise, far too numerous to be described here. Suffice it to say that experience with several hundred made me, of necessity, a fairly adept surgeon and physician. I simply could not afford expensive doctors' fees, nor the burden of having crewmen laid up.

I had some colourful characters among my numerous complements of crew, and one of these is certainly worth a few lines. He was engaged to a girl in one of our loading ports in Chile, and the day before his wedding he followed the lead of Mr Dolittle in *My Fair Lady*, and arrived in the early morning at the home of his bride-to-be in very high spirits indeed, where his bride, beautifully and appropriately decked in white, was ready for the church. However, when the family unanimously refused to allow him to ride to the church on their big pig, he furiously gave his father-in-law a thrashing, slapped his mother-in-law and his intended bride, and went to sea. After a cooling-off period, the penitent sinner returned, and soon after they arrived at the church by conventional means. The wedding took place and they probably lived happy ever after. The boy was clever at smoking the fish we caught while he was on board, and I have heard that he continued in this trade later ashore. During the time he was a member of my crew, he helped me to retrieve one of the anchors of the wrecked English sailing ship *Kynance*. She had drifted ashore on Punta Blanca, near Tocopilla in Chile, in a dead calm in 1895. Endless bureaucracy prohibited the export of iron from Chile, but I managed the matter by obtaining an export licence for scrap iron. This was accepted and I loaded my trophy and took it to Panama, from whence I shipped it to Norway. It now embellishes my garden in Arendal. The original weight was 2,200 kilos, and the export licence indicated 1,980 kilos, a loss of 220 kilos to water and air in the fifty-two years since 1895.

I was now supervising the building of the two sister ships, the *John Wilson* and the *Chilean Nitrate* in Japan. These were being financed by our charterers, who had been so satisfied with my services that their confidence in me had prompted them to finance the new project. I had used every trick in the book on their behalf, and among these, overloading must have been the most lucrative. Incidentally, I did also sign a contract for two general cargo closed shelter-deck ships, which was very fortunate. My financial situation was very strained, and after a few months — the prices for such ships having increased considerably — I sold these two contracts for a good profit. I also became involved in two roll-on/roll-off ships; but this venture failed and reduced the profits I had made on the two contracts by twenty-five per cent — about $200,000.

As a seaman, I cannot profess to be well-versed in the politics of the boardroom. That place of momentous decisions, where contracts are drawn up and signed, after close perusal of the small print of countless specifications, where fortunes can be made and lost among the clauses, memoranda and insertions, where the expertise of far loftier brains than mine conspire to produce a ship, has never really been my scene. Woe betide the man responsible for an error creeping in among the minutiae, for, in the case of gentlemen from the Orient, loss of money means 'loss of face'.

Without going into too much detail, I can relate that I had

had various clauses submitted on memoranda and accepted at the outset of the project for the building of the two new ships at the Tamao Shipyard in Japan. It was therefore with some surprise that I found myself summoned to a meeting with the shipyard directors and their lordships from Tokyo, the heads of the shipbuilding business, newly flown in. It was this august body of eight or nine people who confronted me as I presented myself in the boardroom with a week's stubble on my chin and dirty overalls, coming as I had from closely supervising the work at the yard. I had spent most of my time crawling between plates and girders and bulkheads to check that the welding was to my complete satisfaction. The top brass of the company were not happy. It seems that the demands set out in my three memoranda, although previously accepted, were now proving to be a problem; indeed, if carried out to the letter, they would make the difference between profits and loss for their lordships. I cannot say my heart bled for them, but nevertheless I was prepared to compromise on some smaller details, while remaining adamant on my main provisions.

Now when a European gets excited or tense or simply out of temper, his face may take on a hue ranging from rose to the deepest purple. It is the same with the Japanese, only the shades are from cream to the darkest mahogany. I could feel the temperature rising all round the room as they realized that they were not going to get what they had travelled so far to obtain. Someone along the line had slipped up, and they were in a hole and knew it. Humble-pie is not a well-known dish in Japan; but a more appropriate dessert might be Hara-Kiri.

I rose, making it clear I had nothing further to contribute to the meeting, and excused myself on the ground of pressure of work. The dark countenances were now rather solemn, though one or two contrived a plastic smile. I would hear more in due course, they would approach New York. Little did they realize that *I* was New York, and had they carried out their threat it might well have been me confronting them over the desk.

'My God, John!' my associates commented on my return to New York. 'You've taken these people on and beaten them at their own game!'

I cannot, however, with any decency, refuse to admit that I admire the Japanese honesty. They are straightforward, and the fact that I had 'beaten them at their own game' (when puny

Captain Wilson was supposed to have been defeated in a most disproportionate game, loss of which could have meant famine) did not affect my self-esteem — it only rendered me less tense. I *was* cunning — I had to be — and it was not in my power to extend any further relief to the shipbuilders.

Before proceeding, I must relate a ridiculous affair which challenged a spontaneous bluff.

A Swedish shipmaster was, like myself, supervising the building of a ship in Japan. Before the departure of this vessel, which he was to captain, a little Japanese compass adjuster approached us one day with the curve of compass deviations which he had ascertained for the ship. The curve was undoubtedly correct, but unorthodox in that it was all laid down on the side of the zero line. The Swede, being nearly twice the size of the Japanese, flew into a rage, fixing the poor fellow with red-rimmed, boozy eyes. There suddenly flashed upon me a recollection of my teacher at the Maritime Academy demonstrating such a presentation and explaining how the conventional appearance was obtained simply by moving the zero line. I never understood it, and still don't, but with a knowledgeable air I pointed this out to the adjuster, who immediately understood and smilingly absented himself, while the dumbfounded Swede kept his mouth shut, pretending that I had explained exactly what he had in mind. Our friendship rose to unprecedented heights, as did our celebrations with the Swedish smörgåsbord, aquavit and beer. But I shall always remember the bestial frown he turned upon the son of Nippon — no doubt I saved his life by my intervention. The best thing about it was that the Swede thought the fellow was actually out to cheat him!

Two further encounters should be recorded, both with the same person, Erling Naess, from whom, it will be remembered, I had bought the old *Nortuna*, which gave me so much trouble with its deposits of sludge. In the end I did get some compensation.

Before selling the *Penelope*, I wanted to convert her from coal to oil. Being desperately low on capital, I approached Naess for a modest loan, which he agreed in principal. But I must first go home and draw up a plan showing how repayment would be made and over what time period. I returned the next day with the whole scheme on paper as requested. He scanned it briefly, shook his head and handed it back to me.

'You cannot do this, Captain. It is simply not on.'

'I can and I will!' was my reply; and with that the meeting closed.

At a somewhat later date I had occasion to call on him again. I was very worried that a special subsidy I had from the Americans was about to be withdrawn, and desperately needed reassurance. I took a plane to Tokyo to speak to Erling Naess, who I knew was building ships in Japan. After about an hour in his waiting room, his highness finally condescended to see me. His greeting was a little unexpected.

'How dare you have the effrontery to call on me like this, Captain Wilson?' I was astounded. Was he put out that I had made such a success of a ship he thought no use for anything but scrap? But I may say to his credit that he eventually softened and gave me the assurance I sought regarding the subsidy.

Less significant, but considerably more mutually pleasurable and beneficial from the maritime and personal standpoint, were my meetings with other seafaring men, such as Commodore Bayliss, aboard the *Regina Maris* in New York.

Circumnavigator, Commodore John S. Bayliss, USCG (Ret) was a graduate of the New York Nautical Schoolship *St Mary's*, 1903 and US Coast Guard Academy, 1910. He made four European cruises on the old Sloop-of-War, *St Mary's*, one trip around the world aboard the four-masted British barque *Arrow* and three Alaskan cruises to Nome and Point Barrow on the old Revenue cutter *Bear*. He was Ship Routing Officer, New York in World War I and Captain of Port of New York in World War II. He started the US Coast Guard Identification System and holds many medals, including the Gold Life Saving Medal. He has his Master's licence unlimited for sail and steam.

I met Captain Peter Lohmeyer aboard the German sail training ship *Gorch Foch* and later aboard the three-masted barque *Seute Derne* in Arendal; the late First Sea Lord, Vice-Admiral Sir Michael Le Fanu in London; Captain Adrian Small aboard the *Nonesuch* in Plymouth and later aboard the *Cutty Sark* in Greenwich, where the Cape Horners meet for supper after the Annual General Meeting of the AICH, the Cape Horners' Club, British Section and during the annual Congresses; both Captain Berry of the barque *Endeavour* and the First Sea Lord, Vice-Admiral Sir Victor Smith, aboard the

Regina Maris in Sydney, Australia, during the bicentenary celebrations of Captain James Cook; and a number of Cape Horner Master Mariners and Mates during the yearly Congress in Adelaide. I had the opportunity to visit the Admiralty Building in Whitehall when I met the First Sea Lord, Sir Peter Hill-Norton, and once, also in Arendal, I met Captain Hero Riemer aboard the three-masted topsail schooner *Amphritite*.

Last, but certainly not least, I can always recall to my mind the motley crowd of Mates aboard, and often later on ashore; many of whom became close to me, much as a brother, and the elders dear to me as a father.

I even met a former Master of one of Barbara Hutton's yachts — a marvel of a three-masted sailing ship, crossing skysail yards above the Royals. He was a Norwegian American. I have forgotten his name and that of the yacht. The photo he gave me has since disappeared from my files, but will undoubtedly surface sooner or later. That was in 1966, when I drydocked the *Regina Maris* in Jacksonville, Florida, where we also shipped a new topgallant mast and a mizzen topmast, reminiscent of the westward doubling of Cape Horn. He was a good 'old salt', and the director of Jacksonville Shipyard.

I also met some appalling characters, such as the son of some Caribbean dictator who had been visiting Los Angeles in his father's sail training ship, crewed by some 200 cadets. He had had a real spree in Hollywood, lavishing mink coats and diamond rings on every starlet who wandered his way. Not unnaturally, his father sternly recalled him. The sailing ship was a beauty indeed.

But I must now revert a while to the progress of my new ships in Japan. Supervising the whole process was proving to be an arduous assignment, demanding all my time and attention. I had had to leave the *Nortuna* in the care of my brother at that stage, but later we acquired another master and so were able to cut down on expenses. The builders tried to skimp at every opportunity, but I caught them out. Waving my camera, I warned them that the ships must be properly cleaned before painting, and this should only be undertaken when the weather was suitable. I threatened them that if they tried anything like they had done for a Danish owner they were also working for, I would go and inform him of their perfidy, backing up my testimony with photographs. This had the desired effect, and we got along famously. The result was two beautifully finished ships.

I had to stick my neck out more than once, both for my own benefit and for that of the charterers. The old-style hatches were out of the question, I decided; we must have the new McGregor type, and avoid all that rigmarole with hatch-beams, three sets of tarpaulins, wedges, sealing bars and so on.

My mother launched the two vessels in 1956, and I took delivery of the second one and sailed her out of Japan.

8

Riding High

The big problem now was money. Things were extremely tight and the top men in New York and Chile both began to get cold feet. They both wanted out of the whole scheme. At the very moment when I thought I could rely on their support to get things running in a comfortable and economic way, they were ready to desert. They had, in fact, over-reached themselves. I had to fight the thing through alone, and there was only one way, as I saw it: smuggling.

Already, in the days of the *Nortuna*, I had done some smuggling on a small scale: whisky, cigarettes, nylons, etc. This I now had to increase enormously just to cover my down payments. Where I had previously carried twenty or thirty cases of cigarettes — each case holding fifty cartons and each carton 200 cigarettes — I now handled two or three hundred cases at a time. On one occasion I bought 800 cases from the US Navy at rock bottom prices because they were glad to get rid of them in one deal, and I, of course, made a handsome profit out of that particular arrangement.

Having finally put things on a sound basis, I wanted to retire. Perhaps get that sailing ship I had always dreamed about. Go where *I* wanted to go, free of the confines of the charterers' contracts, free of the strictures of the hard world of business. Most people dream of more money to be won — I just wanted my freedom. I had forgotten what it meant to relax, to take things easy. I had been rushing around loading and discharging at various points around the globe for all too long, driving men and ships to the limit, and for what? To placate the moguls of Wall Street? I was only flesh and blood, after all, and felt I had reached a watershed in my life. I must now retire, but before doing that there would be just one more load of contraband — a really *big* load. Then finish.

Mention must here be made of an episode during a short call at Callao in Peru, where we were discharging part of our cargo. In making out the usual clearance documents for immigration, medical authorities and customs, I began to have misgivings about the quantity of cigarettes I had on board, or rather, those I should declare. Whisky and other contraband I certainly had, but six million cigarettes gave me something of a headache. All those noughts buzzed around my head — nought means nothing, but can make the difference, as Mr Micawber tells us, between misery and happiness. Just check with your bank manager, if you doubt me. Then I lit on the word *carton*. Of course, everyone knows that a carton contains two hundred cigarettes, and these are contained in a larger carton, which holds fifty of the first kind. These larger cartons were what we had on board, six hundred of them — enough tobacco for half the subcontinent.

So I declared six hundred cartons and crossed my fingers. But a minor official caught me out when checking my bonded stores. A claim was levied against the ship for $1,000,000 (those damn noughts again). Although I was insured against such claims, I knew that at best I would be questioned about why I was carrying so many cigarettes, and at worst my ship would be very seriously delayed. However, so important is it to be a member of the *Corps Caballeros* that I was able to settle the matter over a grandiose eight course luncheon with the highest customs officials. My list was acknowledged without further ado, but I thought the attitude of the petty official rather ominous — and I had good reason.

My wife and I had brought a car with us, and now intended to take the opportunity to relax and see the sights of Chile while the contraband was unloaded. I signed off as captain and left the ship in the hands of my Chief Officer. Unfortunately, the unloading was interrupted by the police. The militia are always at the ready in such cases, and shooting quickly broke out, resulting in the deaths of two policemen and two soldiers. That was bad, as it meant the matter would have to be dealt with by a military court. We were three days' journey away, and heard the news of the capture of smugglers north of Valparaiso over the radio, and that the *Chilean Nitrate* was suspected of being the smugglers' vessel. This would be confirmed when the ship arrived in port.

Outside the port the pilot boarded with the usual greeting and no sign of unusual concern. I could not actually ask what I was so eager to know, and he obviously wasn't about to volunteer information.

'How was the voyage down, Captain?' he asked.

'Well, you know . . . cold,' I said.

'Yes?'

'Yes.'

'Oh yes.'

'Tell me, Mr Pilot, did you hear anything about the smugglers at Valparaiso?'

'Yes, it came over the radio. A very big affair there, I believe.'

'Oh, yes?'

'Yes.'

'Hmm.'

And that was that.

This was at the port of Valdivia, where we discharged into lighters. A motor launch took us for a four-hour journey up the river to the city. It was a dismal scene, as there had been an earthquake a year earlier. Many tall buildings had been razed to the ground, and several wrecked ships were to be seen. The captain and my brother accompanied me to the Chief of Customs. The customs clerk struck me as a very unpleasant type. The Chief himself was nervous and tense, with bags under his eyes, and gave me more than one withering stare. The reason I learned later. He was shortly afterwards caught smuggling in a grand style. Perhaps he did not quite fit into a system where a *caballero*, be he a pirate, a bishop or an ambassador — and which is worse, anyway? — is estimated as such. His accomplice got away through bribery, and I was later a guest at their fabulous home, where every item of furniture was an unlawfully imported luxury unequalled in those parts. A pleasant man, he was, as law-breakers must be if they are to get away with it.

Sitting in my hotel over drinks with my wife, and not a little under the influence, what with my name in red headlines and my nerves as tense as steel, I decided it would be better to leave.

'I feel the need to leave Chile just now. In fact, I'll leave tonight, and take only a small suitcase.'

'Well,' she said, 'I'm here for a holiday. I want to stay and see a little.'

'All right,' I said, not sharing her enthusiasm. 'You stay here if you want, or dare, but I think it is not very healthy for me just now.' And I went and arranged a ticket for the flight the same evening.

At that point my wife changed her mind and decided to come with me. I was able to arrange a ticket for her too, and we passed the time until departure over more drinks at my brother's home. As it turned out, we waited rather too long and had to make a mad dash to the airport, only to find the plane already cleared for take-off. Fortunately, even though we had already been paged for the last time, a former crewman of mine, now employed at the airport, recognized me and was able to fix things. We drove right out to the plane, where a ramp was lowered for us, climbed aboard, and away we went.

I flopped into my seat, at the end of my tether, and slept solidly till we arrived in Lima, where in those days it was necessary to stop for fuel. I awoke with the thirst of a camel and a tongue as thick as an old boot. With the other passengers we went 'ashore' to find a bar and pass the time until we were recalled. As we approached the gate, the police asked my wife and myself to step aside . . . This is it, I thought. Now they'll take us back to Chile. But by that stage I was incapable of caring very much what happened. After a while an official returned, saying that everything was in order and we could proceed to the plane. There were no questions and we boarded the plane with light hearts.

I found out that an arrest order had been issued in Santiago five weeks earlier, but they had sat on it in the hope of finding new evidence. Border relations between Peru and Chile were not good at that time, and there could have been a breakdown in the collaboration procedures.

On arrival in New York I telephoned back to my brother. He had driven back from the airport and was in good spirits, if a little tense. Two days later I rang again to hear if there was any more news. My nephew answered and told me that his father had been arrested. The house had been surrounded in the middle of the night, and armed militia had taken my brother, the Master and the Chief Officer to jail in Valparaiso. The following day a policeman had come with the news that his father was being tortured, but that if he could pay a thousand dollars he could get him released.

Somehow, the boy got the money together and paid it over, but of course he never heard any more. A common trick in those parts, and doubtless often still played today. I did my best to reassure my nephew and told him I would send down the best lawyer I could find. I called up my lawyer and told him to go down to Chile immediately.

'Oh, no,' he replied. 'Perhaps next week.'

'Yes?' I said icily. 'Tomorrow morning!'

Then he wanted to take a friend with him, an experienced lawyer who had made a name for himself during the Prohibition. I went at once and procured tickets for them, and in the morning they were on their way.

They managed to have the ship released, and my brother, the Master and the Chief Officer were allowed to go after two months. They were forbidden to leave Chile, however, and when they appealed were told that they could leave if they could hand over the 'big fish'. The 'big fish', of course, lay low in New York. I was sorry that I would not see Chile again — it is a lovely country, with pleasant people. Some years later I received some papers which declared that I was free and that I had been wrongly accused, and that no further action would be taken against me. But somehow I could not bring myself to trust those documents.

The Master managed, by clever argument and copious reference to the ship's charts, to convince the court that he had been outside territorial waters when the 'incident' occurred, and they accepted his story. So, whether or not there had been any smuggling, it had taken place outside Chilean jurisdiction. But I had taken the ship to within three quarters of a mile of the shore, so that the small boats would have the least distance to contend with. I had also supplied a large rubber dinghy to facilitate the transportation of the six hundred cases of cigarettes and all the whisky. The small boats had walkie-talkies and the whole operation was directed from my office and the bridge.

The man in charge of the shore operation is worthy of mention. He was a rough wildcat type with numerous honourable scars. He had once received a pistol shot which went straight through one cheek and out the other, without touching teeth or jawbone: *Galne hunder faar revet skinn* (Mad dogs get torn pelts) as they say. I myself have had my nose broken on three occasions: once by a Polish policeman after a vodka spree in Gdansk; once by a wilful wire rope; and once by a crank-handle. It looks better now than when it started: when things have got as bad as they can, they generally begin to look up.

Referring again to our New York broker, I recall that I traded half of one of my companies for half of one of his. He was a clever man, originally from Bergen, who had taken American citizenship. His company, however, went broke, and I put in a lot of money trying to keep it afloat, but to no avail. The frantic efforts of Hans to raise more capital for his roll-on/roll-off venture led us into some of the loftier regions cf big business, briefly rubbing shoulders with the dynastic tycoons of commerce, finance and shipping. One Jewish financier we contacted went by the name of Truman, and his luxuriously appointed office was eloquent testimony to the success of his calling. He was, I remember, disgustingly fat, and sported the largest diamond ring I had ever set eyes on. When we were comfortably seated before his huge desk and had formally introduced ourselves, he opened negotiations with the command: 'OK, Hans, shoot!' But that particular negotiation came to nothing.

Hans then tried the firm of Webb & Knapp. They had started off in the 1830's selling buttons and thread, but had now grown so enormous that their offer to rebuild Korea after the devastating war there was taken quite seriously. Once again we found ourselves in a beautifully furnished office with every sign of opulence. This time, however, there was a great column in the middle of the floor, which, when the talking was over and a button was pressed, revealed itself to be a lift shaft. We entered a concealed door and were whisked up to a penthouse bar for preliminary drinks served by smartly dressed coloured barmen in the most elegant surroundings. Then a first class luncheon served on damask and silver and crystal and china. And the result? The owner of fifteen skyscrapers and six ocean liners pleasantly showed us the door.

It is hard to say exactly why I put so much effort into trying to save this dicey project. I suppose I should put it down to the devil-may-care attitude which lives in the heart of every simple seaman, and I am no exception. I had the money at the time, so why not?

I still get a good happy feeling when a pile of banknotes lodges in my breast pocket. I have never had a current account or a cheque book, let alone that abominable artifice, a credit card. During all those years when I had nothing to set aside, I acquired the habit of always carrying ready cash, and this system — a godsend, man's best friend — I intend to continue. Do I despise people, men and women alike, pulling out their status symbols, their idols, cheque book and credit card, and complementary identification cards, and proceeding to hold up everyone else in the queue? It is simply ridiculous that these imposters cannot produce a few pounds in ready cash.

I remember all too well the ominous accumulation of unpaid bills and the endless dunning that was our lot in the Great Depression of the 1930's, when we were on the edge of bankruptcy. Could that have influenced my faith in the security of concealed cash? I rediscover again and again how deep-rooted my attitude is when five thousand pounds in my pocket makes me feel I own the whole world. Not a shadow of envy when I read the articles on tycoons and magnates and their measures in billions rather than millions. What do they have that is more satisfying than what I have? However, rather than despise the snobs, whatever meaning one gives to that term, I rather like them and their life of comedy. There are always plenty of lovelies in attendance, affording ample opportunity for stimulating dalliance.

I well remember the confusion of one lady — slip of the tongue? association of ideas? — when she addressed me as Mr Smith. I can still smile at the recollection of an elegant ball in a lovely West-side mansion. The young son of a well-to-do shipowner from the provinces was invited, and considered a good match for the daughter of the house. Although flat broke at the time, my father footed a considerable bill for the most famous and expensive shop in Oslo, William Smith's, for an elegant mantle. This was left in the cloakroom — oh, excuse me, Mr Wilson.

It came to my attention at that stage that many of the sweet young debutantes went horseback riding, and consequently I bought a horse and the necessary equipment, and enjoyed all the better our comings-together after the outings. However, I discontinued this pursuit when the horse threw me off onto a heap of stones and left me with a broken wrist.

Gone are the days when I would frequent the cabaret stage entrances and send nosegays onto the stage. The sweet actresses! I loved their art and skill — especially the latter. I was myself a good-looking charmer in those days. *Sic transit gloria mundi.* Yes, I shall always feel relaxed and happy with a bunch of banknotes. And whenever I feel it slimming down, the uneasy feeling of surfacing unpaid bills hastens me into replenishing my 'saviour'. Not for me the charm of the country house and chicken yard and relaxing in front of the hearth, cows lowing and church bells pealing in the distance!

But back to the shipping ventures. My 'friend' would, he said, make reparation one way or the other, the money would be reimbursed when the time was right. This was the man who had partnered us in the building of the nitrate carriers in Japan, and then contracted two further new ships for me. This time it would be at another ship builder's, and a different type of ship — general cargo vessels, of a similar size to the nitrate carriers.

So I was once again in Japan, arranging specifications and later on selling the contracts. This transaction brought us handsome profits, something to the tune of three quarters of a million dollars.

While I was about the business of getting rid of my partners in the nitrate offices in New York and Santiago, I became acutely aware of some underhand goings-on: irregularities is the word in this case. I had to act quickly, and called a board meeting in New York, which I chaired. The atmosphere was tense, and, as my brother said later, you could have heard a pin drop.

'Hans,' I said, coming straight to the point, 'I will now manage the finances here in the States and in Santiago myself.'

There followed a few moments of absolute stillness, while all eyes focused on our man, whose face slowly drained of colour. The cornered rabbit. He had apparently begun to speculate with our money in another field. There was only one thing he could do to save his face.

'All right,' he said, 'I'll sell my part and quit.'

'I'll take that, Hans,' I said, and the matter seemed to be satisfactorily concluded. But it was not quite so simple, after all.

Our bank account at the Chase Manhattan in New York was attached by Hans, and we had over two hundred cheques returned. Fortunately, my 'lair' had several 'exits', as is very necessary in the hard world of business, especially when one is confronted by sharp practice. I found a little-used exit with the help of my lawyer, and opened another account in another state. As the cheques bounced our reputation plummeted, and we had to write letters by the hundred asking for the forbearance of our creditors, explaining the matter and informing them that all would soon be put right. This in fact soon happened, and we were able to give them all complete satisfaction with very little delay.

The Chase Manhattan Bank was glad to welcome me back as one of their valued depository customers, and wrote us a very warm letter to this effect. Our reputation with them was so good that we had no trouble some years later raising half a million dollars — in fact, I negotiated that particular loan within the space of twenty minutes and without the assistance of my lawyer, who was rather dejected at losing the commission on the transaction!

To return to my brethren with the cold feet in New York and Chile. I saw now that I could no longer rely on them for anything. I decided to buy them out — which was what they wanted.

The New York man was a hard case, and bled me of a quarter of a million dollars before he bowed out, and it was fixed so that he paid the smallest possible amount of tax. The man in Chile was easier. Doubtful as he was about the current venture, he was easily satisfied with a payment of some sixty thousand. I considered myself well rid of them, but the payments had to be made within a fixed time, and if there was any delay they would appropriate the vessels or force me to sell. I accepted the conditions and saved every penny to meet my obligations.

9

Confrontation

One tends to become forgetful with the passage of time. Events
and experiences recede to a dim place in the subconscious, and
time becomes a flickering picture of vague happiness, triumph,
despair, success, bitterness, highlights and low lights — to coin
a phrase — all modified and tempered as the years progress.

This reflection brings to mind a trip we had with the *Chilean
Nitrate* with a cargo of fertilizer, part of which was for delivery
to Holland and the remainder to Sweden. I immediately
foresaw problems ahead for us, on account of the Swedish
boycott of all Liberian registered vessels at the time, and
strongly advised the charterers against sending the vessel into
a Swedish port, but it was to no avail.

We duly arrived in Gothenburg after anchoring up for over
two weeks in the Skaw waiting for the ice to let us through. All
sea marks had been taken in, and would not be set out again
until the area was ice-free. On arrival in the port the stevedores
came on board and discharging got under way, but only a few
tons of cargo had been landed before the unions stepped in and
put a stop to the whole proceedings.

During the time we were held up I was far from idle. I used
the time to carry out a complete refit of the main engine and
auxiliaries, calling in experts from the firm of Burmeister &
Wain. I was therefore in no hurry to get to sea again. I also took
the opportunity for a business trip to Spain and a visit to my
mother in Norway. The charterers, in the meantime, were
frantically trying to contact me, and were never sure of my
whereabouts. But the ship was now brought up to standard after
having become extremely run down, so I had made good use of
the enforced delay.

I was now summoned to a meeting in the sumptuous offices of the International Transportworkers' Federation, where I came face to face with labour leaders, lawyers, union bosses and what not. The proposition was simple: pay up, cede to our demands, and you can sail. Once clear of the port, you can do what you like with the men.

I realized that the cargo of fertilizer would need to be ploughed in before the crop sowing season, and serious delay in unloading it would mean it could not be used until the following year, which could result in a major claim for damages. So I approached the charterers with *my* proposition: I would make my peace with the ITF and draw up a contract for the men which would be to their satisfaction; work would commence and the ship would be free to sail again. The charterers accepted this in all details and I was able to put my $20,000 reward to good use in settling many of the bills which had accrued.

There were also problems with the crew. Any crew problem involves trouble-makers, and these usually have a ringleader. In this situation the ringleader was a nasty piece of work who carried a knife and was not slow to use it. During a routine search of the ship, in which I inspected every cabin on board, this fellow refused to open his door. He only submitted after I had threatened to have the door smashed in and had produced my revolver. I later had to have this man and his cronies repatriated to Chile. I had caught him on the quayside addressing the lady consul with a cigarette hanging from the corner of his mouth. I reminded him in Spanish of his manners. At once his face took fire. If he had not known I was armed, he would have run me through on the instant.

It is worth a mention here that on the occasion of the drawing up of my last charter I had insisted on the insertion of a clause which would protect me against a possible fall in the value of the almighty dollar. The very suggestion prompted a round of derisive laughter from the assembled company. How could a little man like me possibly think of anything so ridiculous? Nevertheless, I stuck by my premonition, or instinct, or call it what you will, and insisted that the clause be inserted. Two years later the dollar plummeted by some forty per cent — a fall which would have spelt a great loss for me, as it did for many others, but for the protective clause in my charter contract.

At the end of that charter I became very uneasy about the

future. Although I hated the idea of being without a ship, I decided to sell. I was just in time. Not long afterwards the market hit rock bottom, and has never recovered. I recall my father's comments from the years long gone, and his long-dead voice still seems to guide me at critical moments. 'Shipping, my boy,' he would say, 'is dangerous business. It's either feast or famine.' He spoke from experience, and he was certainly right.

10

Random Memories

Keeping your memories in order is next to impossible without a diary. My diary is really only a handful of passports, each of which I have kept every time a new one arrived. The first of these, of course, were Norwegian. To a certain degree the same role is filled by the many logbooks from the ships which I have commanded during more than twenty years. However, as my memories draw to a close, several incidents and impressions stand out, and it is these I would like to record here, perhaps not comprehensively, but better some mention than none at all. That will then be about all which may be of interest as far as life from the 1910's to the 1970's is concerned.

My experience with Consuls has generally been disappointing, to say the least, and that was my chief reason for changing from Panamanian to Liberian registry. Consuls usually live right on the outskirts of the towns, entailing expensive taxi journeys and frustrating delays for shipmasters with little time and less money. They demand exorbitant fees and can hold up your ship in port to suit their slightest whim.

I believe that within the plush and panelled walls of Consulates around the world there sit people who can truly be classified as the scum of the earth. One such character charged me for every possible and impossible thing when I arrived in his office. He bore a fine sounding name (which merely confirmed that he was a direct descendant of Spanish pirates). My logbook and papers, all duly stamped, were not enough for him. I happened to have a newspaper with me, which he promptly stamped for ten dollars. This was then increased to twenty dollars, in spite of my protests, because he was now on overtime, and therefore everything had to be doubled!

Luckily, my next trip, via the Straits of Magellan, Brazil and Argentina, was to Liberia, to load iron ore for Philadelphia. It was in Liberia that the idea came to me to change the ship's registry, in the hope of avoiding some of the blood-sucking Consuls. I went ashore in Monrovia to the Ship Registry Office at 80 Broad Street. Though this was nothing but an unpaved lane, it was ironically the very same address used by many shipbrokers in New York. I was informed that the correct place to re-register my ship was in New York, where the High Commissioner for Liberia was to be found. While in Liberia I saw a tribal king from the interior, enjoying a visit to the 'Grand City' with his twenty wives in train.

My crew were all eager to go ashore, despite my warnings of the kind of welcome they could expect. They got no further than the end of the pier before they were involved in a lively brawl, resulting in missing teeth, black eyes, and even a missing part of one ear.

At sea again, I noticed that I had a mosquito bite at the base of the little finger of my right hand. Ten days later I began to shiver and sweat, and I knew I had contracted malaria — the three-day type, also known as 'break-bone fever'. It recurred every three days until I reached Philadelphia. The hospital confirmed my diagnosis and I was furnished with the appropriate medicines for self-treatment at sea, and made a complete recovery.

I would add that after all I did no better under the Liberian flag!

The *Regina Maris* is, in a way, a history of the latter-day clipper. She slid off the stocks at Svendborg in Denmark in 1908, in the well-known yard of Ring-Andersen. I found her, damaged by fire, in a Swedish port, where one of my ships had been boycotted and I had come to settle the matter. Considered a write-off, I bought her from the underwriters for five thousand Swedish crowns. Jury-rigged, I sailed her to Norway for repairs and re-rigging. She was the most beautiful ship, and had had an auxiliary motor installed only when she had already been twenty-four years at sea. I transformed her from a three mast fore-and-aft schooner into a three mast barquentine, and she carried all the flying kites and fancy sails of her famous predecessors.

Rebuilding a fifty-eight year old oaken ship to the highest

class in Lloyds as a sailing cargo vessel, and so conjuring up a clipper from the past, proved difficult and expensive. Danish oak was shipped to Norway and the countryside scoured for old carpenters and riggers. With bottom coppered and masts stepped, the ship of the past rose again. Two hundred and sixty deadweight tons, she drew a graceful twelve-foot draught. She had a carved figurehead and scrollwork at the bow and a lovely rounded stern. Bronze images of cats adorned the catheads of this little Queen of the Seas. The Captain's quarters and those of the crew were of high standard, and we lacked nothing from galley to medicine chest.

I had long nurtured the ambition of conducting, in my capacity as Sea Captain, the wedding of my then youngest daughter at sea. My investigations revealed that a wedding conducted at sea by the master of a ship was not acceptable in law. The *Regina Maris* was then registered in Valletta, Malta, at a time when that country was in the process of becoming independent of Great Britain. I learned from our Maltese agents that such a wedding would similarly not be 'good in law' in Malta. Simultaneous confirmation came from lawyers in Norway and the USA.

Nothing daunted, I put to sea, and on August 11th 1966, at three in the afternoon, with *le d'Ouessant* about sixty miles abeam, the ship was hove to with sails up in leech, and buntlines. That sunny afternoon my daughter and her fiancé were united in marriage by me. The uniformed crew attended; stair carpets were rolled out over the deck plants, and the ceremony proceeded according to plan.

My son conducted his sister, the bride, on to the deck. She was dressed completely in white, with a nice nosegay — a rare spectacle aboard a sailing ship on the high seas. The bridegroom followed in immaculate dinner jacket. I delivered an address with text from the Methodist Minister's Manual, and exchanged rings for the young couple. I reserved for myself the honour of opening the first bottle of champagne to toast the newly-weds. The marriage was entered in the logbook in the presence of two witnesses, and the entry was officially authenticated and signed by the British Consul in Lisbon, and later filed with the proper authorities in Valletta, Malta.

From Lisbon, I informed our agents in Valletta that I had received their letter, but — alas! — too late. I then suggested that they contact the proper authorities with a view to trying to influence them to establish a precedent by changing the statutes, as a demonstration of their new-found independence. Six months later I received a letter informing me that the Law of Malta had been changed with regard to marriages at sea, and that henceforth it was legal for a shipmaster to conduct a marriage ceremony on the high seas. The marriage certificate is an authenticated abstract of the logbook, which is entered in the Registry of Malta, where a copy may be obtained. Shades of the old 'Lex Wilson' of 1949 in Norway . . . .

I should mention that my granddaughter, born on November 17th 1967, bears the name of Astrid Regina. And a measure of the attachment felt by the crew for the ship can be seen in the names three of *their* daughters bear: Silvia Regina, Hedda Regina and Kathrine Regina.

You can find more of the *Regina Maris* story in my book *Wooden Walls to Distant Shores — the Regina Maris Story*, but I would like to follow this wedding story with an episode of quite another nature.

During my second voyage to Australia by way of Cape Horn, I was dismasted in the Atlantic, south of the Cape Verde Islands. On Monday, October 13th, 1969, at 09.00 local time, a thunderbolt struck the foremast, which broke in three or four places and went over the starboard bow, dragging the main topmast and part of the lower- and mizzen-topmasts along with it. A shocking sight greeted me when I came on deck: some eighteen of the twenty-five sails we had set were in horrible confusion, partly on deck and partly overboard. We had a lightning conductor from the foremast truck, but why had it not protected us? I was the only one who knew that when the new, taller, topgallant mast had been shipped in Jacksonville, Florida, in 1967, the lightning conductor was too short, and a piece had been added. The conductivity of the joint was inadequate.

The ship was towed back to Norway for a refit. We were bound for Sydney to attend the Bicentenary celebrations of the voyages of Captain James Cook. Time was getting short, so I changed the itinerary by doubling the Cape of Good Hope and running down across the Indian Ocean. On the return voyage, in addition to marvellous visits to Papete on the beautiful island of Tahiti and to Pitcairn Island, we had a mutiny. The crew

refused to return by way of Cape Horn in winter time. After
landing seven men in Peru, I had run out of time, and had to
return by way of the Panama Canal and Curaao, where I put
the ship in dry dock. Then a hurricane in the English Channel
in December 1970 brought me to within an inch of disaster, and
that was my last long voyage under sail. I sold the ship and
sailed her down the North Sea to Holland to deliver her to her
new owners. I arrived home two days before Christmas, and
that was the end of my eight years as owner/master of a sailing
ship, following the unbroken tradition of my great-grandfather,
grandfather, and father, all master/owners of steamships.

I have acquired many things in the course of my travels:
diplomas, medals, a knighthood — you name it.

During the harassing years with the old *Nortuna* — she was
approaching thirty-five years of age at the time — I carried a
cargo of grain to Brazil. On arrival, part of the cargo was found
to have been spoiled by sea water. My agents in New York
wanted a plausible explanation for the benefit of the
underwriters. Being rather depressed and not a little
intoxicated at the time, not to mention furious at the whole
business, I sent back the following cable, which may have done
something to my reputation among the shipbrokers in Broad
Street:

'Corrosion fuckit Wilson.'

That might indeed have been what induced Mrs Evenson,
secretary to the manager in the firm I used when I had doubled
Cape Horn in the barquentine years later, to say: 'My
congratulations. I always felt you were a seaman
extraordinary!'

It must have been in 1949 that I found myself in New Orleans
with the old coal-burning *Penelope*. I took the notion to
redecorate my salon. Through my agents I was introduced to a
remarkable man who was an artist of the highest class, as well
as an accomplished musician. Interior decoration was his
business, and he soon led me downtown to an antique dealer
where we viewed some maritime artefacts. He suggested that a
fine mahogany table would go admirably together with a couple
of ship pictures, and I very much agreed with him, even though
they were somewhat beyond my budget. I had given him the
rough dimensions of my salon, but had, perhaps, exaggerated
a little, as an enthusiastic captain might well do. However,

when he later came aboard, and saw how small was the accommodation I had, his interest fizzled out. This little episode is worth a mention if only for the fact that I met a group of his friends, who could well be described as well-to-do bohemians. They were an interesting and talented bunch. I recall an impromptu concert that he gave at the grand piano, where I had a seat of honour at the front of a group of enthralled listeners. With hindsight, I believe his sexual orientation may have been a little deviant, but I cannot be certain. He did manage to get me to drop the woman I had at the time while he showed me around the town, including the well-known Lafitte's Blacksmith's Shop, which is now quite a fashionable bar and restaurant, and also the elegant 'Court of Three Sisters', built with artistic tiles made by the slaves of former decades. At the Blacksmith's Shop I explained how we drank a whisky soda — a tall glass with three measures of whisky and filled with soda. This they enjoyed so much that the drink became known as a 'Captain John'.

I returned some years later on something of a sentimental journey, hoping to renew my acquaintance with these friendly people and taste again the drink they had named after me. My order for a 'Captain John' was met with blank stares from the bar. The episode, the people and the drink had all faded into the mist of time. I ordered a triple whisky with a large soda and drank it in nostalgic solitude before taking my leave. I never went back.

Flippancy rarely pays off in such a pleasant manner as once happened to a party of my friends and myself. We were in a happy state of inebriation and for several days had repaired our hangovers in a most pleasant bar in the beautiful Hotel Princess in Hamilton, Bermuda. The drink we settled on was a Tom Collins, and, being the ringleader, I daily repeated my order with 'Let's say hello to Mr Collins'; whereupon the drinks were brought. On the last day, however, in place of the drinks, a very pleasant and cordial gentleman, in fact the manager of the hotel, appeared in front of us. Introducing himself as Mr Collins, he invited our party to a Tom Collins on the house. This was cheerfully accepted, and I believe Mr Collins, well-bred as he was, pretended to remember me from a previous visit! As it happened, this was my first call at this charming hotel, but hopefully not the last.

11

Feast And Famine

I cannot resist the temptation to insert a laconic synopsis of some ups and downs in the feast and famine course of my life:

1. Imprisoned by the German occupation forces and sent to Germany for eighteen months' hard labour.
2. At the end of the war I bought a small steamship of some 5000 DWT.
3. Annoyed by the government in Norway, I decided — out of spite — to emigrate.
4. A clearing-out sale of my ship left me stranded in the USA during the depression.
5. Bought a twenty-nine year old steamship from Erling Naess. A tremendous slice of luck enabled me to run this old-timer successfully, with numerous 'near calamities'. I was to have it — Kismet!
6. Eighteen months' sojourn in Japan supervising the building of my two new motor ships after negotiations for long term charters.
7. Made a precipitated retreat from Chile when my last 'Grand Style' smuggling venture failed — in the hour of peril indeed.
8. Retired, I bought a three masted barquentine of 260 DWT — 100 feet waterline — and during the following six years sailed her round the world by way of Cape Horn and the Cape of Good Hope. The ship was registered by Lloyds of London, a sailing cargo ship with loadline for Winter North Atlantic and myself as Master.

Upon the first voyage of some sixteen months doubling Cape Horn, I presented myself to the Director of Shipping and Navigation in Oslo and requested that my Master's Licence for steam and motorships be extended to include sailing ships. In this I was successful, although my sea-service in sail should rightly have preceded my signing on as Master of a sailing ship!

And I may as well admit here and now that rather than five years 'before the mast', as quoted in my *Curriculum Vitae* — which otherwise is correct — I only had five months at sea before entering the Merchant Marine Academy.

A diverting appendix I must add. On July 19th 1967, in St Malo, I was accepted an 'Albatross' (a ship captain having doubled Cape Horn in a commercial sailing ship) by Captain Leon Gautier ('Grand Mat' (President) of *The Association Amicale Internationale des Capitaines au Long Cours Cap-Horniers*, Saint Malo) and the Board, my Log Book having been inspected and signed by Captain Gautier and countersigned by his General Secretary, Captain Louis Louvet, during a meeting on board the *Regina Maris*. My brother observed sarcastically: 'I daresay that the button which you now can display is the most expensive one in maritime history.' I reciprocated with a sardonic smile.

9. Gave a grand cocktail party in Rio de Janeiro, attended by the Princess Ragnhild — Mrs Lorentzen and her husband, together with their son Haakon, grandson of the late King Haakon VII. Other guests included the Norwegian Ambassador and their friends.

10. Met King Peter II of Yugoslavia in his apartment in the Waldorf Astoria Hotel in New York. He made me a Knight of the Order of Saint John of Jerusalem. I was also awarded the Royal Yugoslav Commemorative War Cross — 1941-5.

During the time in New York I was also elected Member of the Explorers' Club.

11. In Oslo I was decorated with the Cape Horner Medal — AICH. Later I had an audience with HM King Olav V in the Royal Palace. The King himself graced the ship with a personal visit to the *Regina Maris* to muster the crew and meet prominent members of the Cape Horn Club, of

which he is the Patron in Norway.

12.   After an official reception in Arendal by the town dignitaries, the Burgomaster, the Chief of Police, the Senior Officers' Club, and others, the Burgomaster gave the mayoral welcome home. I reciprocated by throwing a Grand Barbecue. I had a Mexican crew member who could undertake to roast nine lambs.

13.   I showed a two-hour colour movie film of the first voyage, firstly in Arendal and then in Oslo. Prominent people from both cities and representatives of the press attended.

14.   Showed the film in Oslo for the Royal Norwegian Yacht Club. The showing was attended by the Patron, HM King Olav V and HRH Crown Prince Harald. The King was filmed during his visit to the *Regina Maris*. The Crown Prince took me in to the

15.   subsequent dinner.
I was awarded the Medal of St Olav, and granted another audience with HM King Olav V, after our voyage to Sydney, where I represented the Royal Norwegian Yacht Club during the Bicentenary Celebrations of Captain Cook's rediscovery of Australia's east coast. The KNS gave the Royal Sydney Yacht Squadron an elegant old silver cup. For services to the Australian Section of *The Association Amicale Internationale des Capitaines au Long Cours, Cap Horniers* (Cape Horners Australia), I

16.   was elected Honorary Life Member.
And then — five weeks in custody in my own home town of Arendal for alleged tax evasion! But I was released with my honour still bright. Indeed, I can claim that I did have some honour in my own country. But should a cobbler not stick to his last? That proverb brings to mind how my birth certificate was interpreted in Panama: my father's profession was translated from Shipowner to Shoemaker!

12

A Diversion

In truth, I must here deliberate on the lawyers of my native town and cannot help pulling their legs. During an absence of a couple of years I left my affairs with one of them, with instructions to pay bills of all kinds. Upon checking his accounts I discovered disbursements to an unknown fellow, a considerable amount of money. Upon my requesting an explanation it transpired that some cheat had got scent of my arrangement and at intervals came to the lawyer's office, presenting bills for work allegedly done for me. These bills were promptly paid without any check at all. The matter went to Court and the man was sentenced to a term in jail and to repay the money, which, of course, I never received. Surprisingly, I also never received an explanation or excuse from the lawyer. Well, then came the alleged exodus of ratepayers, attended to by his successor. I had carefully supplied xerox copies of my wife's and of my own passports in order to prove that I had not resided in Norway beyond the permitted 180 days in any one year and was not a taxpayer. Norway was not my place of residence as regards taxation. In court, the lawyer for the Collector of Revenue shuffled the two passports and my 'defender' never noticed that my wife's stay in Norway was added to that of my own, thus exceeding 180 days. Then I suggested cessation, whereupon all my mail and other matters were under control of the liquidator. *Inter alia*, all mail addressed to me was to be opened. However, a mislaid letter in my post office box addressed to a foreign firm was unscrupulously opened as well — with no reward — but such a breach of the Postal Convention incurred a prolonged term in jail. No protest from my 'defender'.

I gave instructions to a Law Firm to institute a judicial examination. I quote from a cutting:

> '. . . is herewith authorized to initiate any appropriate lawsuits against Mr Ulf Onsrud, Attorney at Law, of Arendal, Norway, and Mr Madsen, tax collector, of Arendal, Norway, on the grounds of unauthorized opening of mail.'

The lawyer for the Public Prosecutor wrote a letter to the Liberian Ship Register in Monrovia — he knew I had some kind of connection with both Panamanian and Liberian Ship Registers. The result of his intelligent efforts was a polite reply from Monrovia, Liberia, stating that some company by the name of 'Oceanline' or 'Ocean Transport' had indeed been registered, but long ago expunged, and the name J.A. Wilson had never been registered.

I gratefully acknowledged receipt of their communication with the enclosed copies of Onsrud's letter — and their reply. This is indicative, in the extreme, of the naivety of the contestant. Now, to crown their failures, after the passage of years, during which I had had every opportunity I could have wished for to conceal evidence, I was remanded in jail on the pretext of not affording me any possibility to 'destroy evidence'. After a few weeks the local newspaper wrote — quote: 'Now they keep Wilson so long in custody that he shall "fall a martyr".' My 'defender' did nothing worth mentioning by way of defence, but what is worth mentioning is that the brother of the 'famous' lawyer for the Public Prosecutor was a former Chief of Police, and I was inclined to think that the two had hatched a plan — to demoralize me behind bars. Only they did not take into account that I was already a 'seasoned jailbird' from a worse environment in Germany during the war.

Incidentally, I had difficulties in keeping my bodyweight down, and used the six weeks custody to reduce some three kilos in spite of the fact that they had apparently arrested a French Chef who worked in the kitchen of the prison. His food tempted me sorely, and even more so small flasks of whisky which I was offered by occasional visitors — and which I refused.

Well, everything has an end, and a pudding has two. I did

celebrate when I was let out — colours flying. I invite humorous comments. Myself, I can only scorn, despise and detest the parties involved, their expertise and the environment. I would certainly not descend to offer an opinion on the pack, embittered as I am, indeed. I have even used a lawyer from Arendal in New York — first generation immigrant — proudly presenting himself as a 'Wall Street Lawyer'. He was the least expensive lawyer I could find at the time — and so learned that a cheap lawyer usually, if not always, becomes expensive. After several blunders I at last told him that I would like to settle accounts.

He took this last occasion to charge me in the grand style of Wall Street indeed. I was in a fix but had to put a brave face on it. However, soon afterwards (I lived in Denmark at the time) I received a bill for £3,000 from a London lawyer for legal assistance in buying a property in Denmark. I had instructed my New York lawyer to undertake this transaction for me — and refused to pay the bill. I had never been asked to authorize the use of a London lawyer.

The 'Wall Street Character' sued me, and in the Court of Justice in Denmark I drew attention to the fact that the registered Owner of the Property was my nephew — John Aage Wilson, born in 1949. That was the end of the prosecution, and with the pleasant feeling of having carried the day, I laughed up my sleeve.

Before I continue, I would like to include some details about the Order of St John of Jerusalem. All lifeboats bear the Maltese Cross — it is the central motif in lifeboat organizations, not only in Norway but in the lifeboat flags of all countries associated with the International Lifeboat Federation. And why the Maltese Cross? It would perhaps be of interest here to quote at length from Enrle Bradford's article on the long and fascinating history of the Knights of St John, an Order founded in the eleventh century, whose members cared for pilgrims travelling to the Holy Land. In later years the order declared war on all unbelievers and, according to the author, became a combination of pirates and Samaritans. Today, these 'good Samaritans' are responsible for good works all over the world. The article was written some years ago, but is still an up-to-date account of the Order.

Malta's Knights of St John — The Knights of Goodwill, by Ernle

Bradford.

A few years ago in Rome, when I was carrying out some research on the Order of St John, a librarian suddenly handed me a little brown folder. The title surprised me: 'Press Release, Via Condotti, Palazzo di Malta, 17th December 1969'.

I read on: 'Three young volunteer members of the St John's medical team, the German "Hilfsdienst", working at the An Hoa hospital, have died in a North Vietnamese prison camp. Two others are prisoners . . . '

I later learned that the German branch of the Order had maintained a group of forty-five doctors, nurses and health workers in Quang Nam Province since 1966. They had provided help to more than 200,000 Vietnamese from both north and south over a period of three years.

In March 1980, the Vietnamese authorities forced the organization to limit its activities and provide aid to South Vietnamese only — a case of blatant discrimination. The Germans were withdrawn, although not until they had trained a number of Vietnamese to take over and run the hospital. By this time, ten of their members, all young German volunteers in a war which did not concern them, were either dead or missing. Their only aim was to provide relief for the sick and injured, as Knights of St John have done since the early eleventh century.

The Hospitaller Order of St John of Jerusalem, of Rhodes and of Malta is the oldest Order still existing today, and the fourth oldest Christian Order ever. It was founded by some merchants from Amalfi who, like many other Amalfians, transported passengers by sea. They decided to open a hospital in Jerusalem as a service to their customers. At the time it was regarded as a kind of 'insurance' if the carrier could also provide the passengers with medical aid during the journey. From these small beginnings emerged one of the most powerful Knightly Orders the world has ever known.

The founder, today known as Holy Brother Gerard, was the leader of the Jerusalem hospital, effectively the only hospital in the whole of Jerusalem, when the first wave of Crusaders stormed the city in 1099. Following this, the founding of the Christian kingdoms of Jerusalem, Palestine and Syria led to an increase in the stream of pilgrims to the Holy Land.

The hospital expanded and in the twelfth century the Pope

took the Order under his own personal patronage and approved its official foundation as the Order of St John. The Papal Bull may be seen exhibited in the library at Valetta in Malta, where the Knights of St John later had their main stronghold. The character of the organization, originally founded simply to aid the poor and afflicted, rapidly changed. Brother Gerard's successor pointed out to the Pope that the pilgrims' route lay under constant threat of attack by the Saracens, and that it was no longer enough merely to offer succour to the sick and injured — pilgrims on the road should also be protected from attack. The Pope approved of this idea of protecting the travellers, which in practice was the same as attacking the Mohammedans, and the military wing of the Order of St John was born.

The men who formed this military wing, later described as 'the most remarkable religious army the world has ever known', were mostly younger sons of the noble families of Europe.

Every member of the Order, warrior and priest alike, took a vow of poverty, chastity and obedience.

However, contemporaries relate that the members often lived a life of overwhelming luxury and splendour, preaching the gospel of poverty rather than following it, and were constantly bickering among themselves. When the last Christian stronghold fell to Islam at the end of the thirteenth century, the Knights Hospitallers were forced to leave the Holy Land, first for Cyprus and later for Rhodes, which they captured from the Byzantine Emperor in 1309. True to their original calling, the first thing they did was to open a hospital for the care of the poor and the sick.

Here they found a new enemy, not the Saracens, but the Turks, who had also converted to Islam. The Turks were determined to be the mightiest power in the Orient, and were thus a serious threat to European supremacy. However, the Knights did not stand idly by. Together with the native inhabitants of Rhodes and slaves taken from Turkish ships, they raised mighty defences around the island — defences which are today considered by many to be among the architectural pearls of the Mediterranean.

At the same time, the Order itself underwent a period of change. Firmly entrenched as they were behind their mighty bastions, with no other enemy than the sea around them, they began to look outwards. The Turkish ruler's ships passed them every day. What was more natural than that they should become pirates? Christian corsairs, of course. The Pope himself had commanded them to wage war against 'unbelievers' wherever they found them. Through a strange metamorphosis the foot soldiers and cavalry turned themselves into some of the greatest marine warriors in history.

Even though the Knights of St John, with the Pope's blessing, regarded their own activities as supremely praiseworthy, the Turks considered them nothing but a band of pirates. The Knights were in open warfare with all Mohammedans. They were also recognized as an independent state with the same right to declare war, sue for peace and establish diplomatic relations as every other state. Even in our day, the Order is recognized as a sovereign state, and has full diplomatic relations with thirty-seven countries. In fact, if the Order could win the support of a sufficient number of countries, it would be entitled to a seat in the United Nations.

At the end of the fifteenth century, the Turkish Sultan Mehmet II led a comprehensive attack against the island fortress by sea and land. Most of the island was razed and the town of Rhodes was laid under siege. However, the Turks were forced to retreat, with enormous losses.

The Knights of St John were based on the island for two centuries, and were able to perfect the Order's remarkable international structure. It was divided into eight provinces, or *langues*, based on the most important countries at the time: Aragon, Auvergne, Castile, England, France, Germany, Italy and Provence — an international constellation with a dominant French element. Each separate *langue* had its own duties and each was responsible for a particular task of defence. The main language was French — the *lingua franca*.

The end came forty years after the first siege. Sulaiman the Great, the greatest of all the Turkish sultans, whose armies swept through Europe to the very walls of Vienna, was determined to pluck out this thorn in his side. After a siege which lasted six months and cost the lives of thousands of men, he succeeded. The Knights of St John were forced to sue for peace and spent the next seven years wandering from one Royal European court to the other, without a home of their own. This state of affairs lasted until Emperor Charles V decided that it would be useful to have an imperial garrison in the province of Sicily. The Order of St John was given the island of Malta against a symbolic rent of one trained falcon each year.

Malta was a barren contrast to the green and fertile island of Rhodes, and was not particularly attractive to the Knights, but on one point they were all agreed — it had the finest harbours in all the Mediterranean. The peninsula in the part of the island now known as the Grand Harbour had a tiny fishing village and a crumbling old fort. This was the spot! Here they would build a new Rhodes!

In the course of only a few years they established their defences around 'Birgu' ('The Town'). They built a large fortified castle at the outskirts and a smaller one at the end of the peninsula. The Knights were well aware that they could be attacked again, and one of the first buildings to come under cover was a large hospital.

In spite of the fact that the Order received revenues from its properties throughout Europe, money was still a problem. The new defences were a constant financial drain. 'The Caravan' was soon re-established. In other words, swift galleys swept up and down the coast attacking Turkish merchant vessels.

The Sultan soon realized that the Order now represented an even greater threat than when it had been based on Rhodes. At the age of seventy, he decided he had had enough.

His attack on Malta in 1565 has gone down in the annals of warfare. Against a Turkish force of 30,000 men and 200 ships, the Knights of St John could muster no more than 9,000 men, mostly Maltese and Spaniards, under the leadership of a few hundred Knights. The siege lasted from spring to autumn, and the cannons could be heard in Sicily, 100 kilometres away. Sulaiman's defeat at Malta was one of his few military failures, but without doubt his most serious. Church bells rang from town to town throughout Europe to celebrate the happy outcome.

During the centuries which followed, the Knights continued to pursue their two main callings, that of Samaritans and sea-borne warriors. A combination of donations to the Order and booty from Turkish ships enabled them to continue their building on the island. It became an architectural treasure chest, and the beautiful fortified town of Valletta, named after a Grand Master, raised its head from its rocky bed north of the

Grand Harbour.

This small island flourished and became one of the wealthiest and most elegant places in Europe. Many a traveller has gazed with wonder on the walls of Valletta as they lift themselves above the blue Mediterranean — a town of splendour and excitement.

The members of the Order continued to follow their original calling of caring for the sick in the Great Hospital in Valletta. All Europe marvelled at this hospital, with its 170-metre long roof over the main building alone. Treatment was freely available to all, Mohammedans and Christians alike, and patients were served on silver platters by the Knights themselves.

Problems arose during the course of the eighteenth century. Of course, there had always been troubles of one sort or another, which is hardly surprising when a large number of hot-blooded young noblemen live under the same roof.

The main reason for the disintegration of the Order was the state of France, swept by Revolution and new ideas. Since the majority of the Knights were French, they became a regular fifth column within the main Order. With the dissolution of the French monarchy, and the confiscation of the properties of the nobility in France and in other countries conquered by Napoleon, the economic foundation of the Order crumbled. Property and fortunes fell into the hands of the public authorities and the financial well ran dry. When Napoleon paid the island a visit on his way to Egypt and demanded its capitulation, the unconquerable walls of Valletta 'fell' at last. The Order and the Knights were once again driven from their home.

Rome was to be their next home, in the 'Palazzo di Malta', donated by one of their members. The Order's crusading warriors had long since faded into history, and the members concentrated on their original call of aiding the sick and needy. Their income was modest and their properties few, but still the standard, with its 'white cross of peace on the blood-red battlefield', waved stubbornly over the Palazzo di Malta — as it does to this day.

Anyone visiting the Palazzo today, behind the noisy Via Condotti and the hippie-filled Piazza di Spagna, will notice the Maltese Cross crowning the lion's head fountain in a courtyard more peaceful than most other places in this busy twentieth century.

The first impression confirms everything one has heard about the Order — that it is an exclusive club for Roman Catholic noblemen. But this impression soon recedes. Behind the large, noble halls filled with mementoes of the Order's 900-year history is a totally different world, more reminiscent of a modern shipping company or import-export firm than a unique relic of a bygone age.

Everyone I met seemed able to speak three or four languages, a fact which would hardly have surprised the ancient Knights. What would have surprised them, however, is that these languages are no longer spoken from one bastion to another, but through an international communications' network to all four corners of the earth.

The Grand Chancellor himself is a true representative of the Order's international character. His title goes back to ancient days, but in reality he is the Prime Minister of this little state. He looks like an efficient businessman, which he is, since he was also vice-president of Seagrams in Canada.

Quintin Jeremy Gwyn is of Irish extraction, but was born in England and has lived in Canada for many years. He became a Knight of the Order in 1950 as one of the founders of the Canadian branch. As he points out, this was an entirely natural step for a Roman Catholic Canadian, considering the close relationship which had existed between the Order of the Knights of St John and Canada since the old days of the French regime. Indeed, the very first governor of 'New France' was himself a Knight of St John.

The present head of the Order has a twinkle in his eye and seems far removed from the pompous holy brothers of days gone by. Questioned as to whether he had genuinely joined the Order for reasons of historical significance, he replied:

'Any serious person, and I expect that most of us would like to be serious at some time or other, is bound to feel dissatisfied with the thought of nothing but his own career in the long run. From time to time most people would consider the possibilities of doing something, however little, to make a personal contribution towards the fight against poverty in the world.'

I hinted that the Order itself is somewhat of an anachronism in the twentieth century.

'Not anachronistic, but bound by traditions. We are, in fact, so traditional that we find ourselves back where we started in 1099. The military side of the Order ceased to exist many years ago. We are once again the Knights Hospitallers of St John.'

Later I spoke to Carl Wolfgang Graf von Ballestrem, a German lawyer. With his title of Hospitaller he presides over all the Order's health and hospital activities. These activities are spread throughout the world and cover many fields, from treatment and convalescence stations for the lepers of Africa, South America and Polynesia to ambulance units in Germany and Ireland, hospitals in Italy, research clinics, and field units which can be flown out to areas hit by catastrophe anywhere in the world. For example, when Pakistan was hit by cyclones and floods in November 1970, the Order immediately placed five million lire at the disposal of the Pakistani government. A further five million was rapidly collected and 290 crates of antibiotics and other medicines were sent to Bengal. Following the 1970 Peruvian earthquake, a group of seventeen helpers worked in the area for six weeks. By the time they left they had trained Peruvian personnel well enough to take over the field hospital and equipment left behind.

Today the Order has about six hundred Knights as members. About fifty of them are 'professional Knights' — that is, they have taken a vow of poverty, chastity and obedience. Other members of the Order, probably the majority, are married, and many of their wives are Dames of the Order. Women have been eligible to join the Order for hundreds of years, and there are even nuns who bear the Maltese Cross on their habits. Among these are the nuns who work in the Hospital of St John and St Elizabeth in London.

As well as the Knights themselves, there are thousands of volunteers all over the world who contribute their time and skills with no remuneration to aid the Order in its activities. A doctor, for example, can help in his own way, or a lawyer, or an architect. Or, indeed, any young man or woman, even without special qualifications, such as the young Germans who died in Vietnam, who believes in the eternal truths and ideals of the original founders of the Order.

Today the Order's finances have a more solid foundation than in the nineteenth century. The Order has emerged from the shadowy existence of a 'club for antique noblemen'. In 1968 the Order gave the first press conference in its history, and since then Vittoria de Sica has made a television documentary on its activities. In answer to questions posed by an Italian journalist as to what he, a declared radical, had to do with so aristocratic a company, de Sica replied: 'They carry out true works of charity, and anyway, Christ himself was the first socialist!'

The members of the Order, many of them millionaires, make an important contribution to its finances. Apart from this, each member has to pay a fee, the same as would be the case in any other club. This contribution is still known as the 'fee of passage', in memory of the distant days when each pilgrim to the Holy Land should pay his passage before he boarded the ship. Apart from this, each member has to pay an annual subscription based on income — not all members are wealthy.

On the other hand, each individual Knight is welcome to contribute whatever sum he wishes over and above his subscription. I have heard of one Knight who, in addition to his not inconsiderable annual contribution, came to the Palazzo di Malta and deposited 1,000,000 lire each Christmas Day, to be distributed among Rome's poor.

Since the order is sovereign and independent, it is ruled by its own Count, at the moment an Italian 'professional Knight', His Honourable Highness Fra Angelo de Mojana. He is the highest-ranking layman in the Roman Catholic Church. In fact, almost all Knights are on first-name terms with the Cardinals and other members of the Roman hierarchy. 'Our relations with the Vatican are excellent and very close,' I was told.

Close, certainly, but not so close that the Order is under the control of the Vatican. That was something the Grand Masters fought strongly against. The greatest of them all, La Valette, even politely refused a Cardinal's hat after his brilliant efforts and contributions to victory during the siege of Malta. As Grand Master of the Order of St John, he was the equal of any Cardinal, and he preferred to keep it that way. He wished to keep his independence.

Today, throughout the world, the Order of St John continues to contribute to the relief of sickness and poverty. This is all the more remarkable when one considers that all efforts are personal and privately financed.

The Order is a unique survivor from the days of the Crusades, a survivor which, to use Darwin's term, has 'adapted itself'. In a way, it is as if a pterodactyl should suddenly appear in our skies and show itself capable of flying a jet engine! The long-haired members of the Order who fought the Mohammedans from their bases on Rhodes and Malta would hardly recognize their well-dressed, business-like modern successors. All the same, I think that their founder, Brother Gerard, would have given them his blessing.

Today the Maltese Cross, the symbol of the centuries-old activities of the Order of St John, is commonly used as the symbol for life-saving organizations in countries associated with the International Lifeboat Federation.

The Monastery at Rygge in Østfold became the seat of the Order of St John in Norway. It housed both a monastery and a hospital from about 1190 until 1532, when the King confiscated the property for the crown. Today only a few broken walls remain standing.

For a full account of the Order, see pages 426-439 inclusive of the book *The Messianic Legacy* (1986) by Michael Baigent, Richard Leigh and Henry Lincoln.

13

From My Memorandum Book

And so, back to my narration. A circle closed: a small-scale start and a small-scale finish. But I must recall my first, second and third homecomings to Norway with *Regina Maris*. I made a point of always having the ship abundantly stocked with assorted wines and spirits, and on my arrival at Oslo from Cape Horn some fifteen cases of the best Scotch whisky were stowed in my salon benches, precisely where HM King Olav V sat during his visit aboard prior to my audience at the Royal Palace. The rest was located in various cupboards and toilets around the ship, and only a small part of this was declared, either in Oslo or in Arendal, where I laid the ship up in winter quarters. In Arendal I told the Customs and Excise men that I wanted to land my 'bibbables', and they duly came aboard and checked them out in accordance with my declaration. Much to my surprise, they found four bottles of cognac in excess of my statement. When they offered to recount, or to keep the bottles in custody, I told them I would 'cut the Gordian knot', whereupon I smashed the four bottles into the sea — a right queenly libation to the anchorage of the 'Regina Maris. When the Customs men had their invoice for dues and duty paid, they left, and I proceeded to discharge the declared and undeclared boxes.

On my second arrival home — to Kristiansand — I declared nothing, and on one lovely moonlit night brought a rich haul home to my cellar in Arendal.

Now, on my third and last return — again in Kristiansand — I made a complete declaration: righteousness itself. I informed the Customs and Excise of my intention to bring ashore all the wines and spirits. Having paid the truly

113

exorbitant total of duty and dues, I loaded it all onto a truck the following day, and was ready to drive off when the Customs search-party — endearingly known as the 'Black Gang' in Norway — swooped upon us, checking everything aboard and ashore from A to Z. Unfortunately, one of the crew members had put two cases of beer on the truck, which were immediately confiscated. The Chief of Customs, a gnome-like old goat, reported me to the police, and although he did not ask me to pay duty on the beer, he requested the police to summon me for a serious reprimand. I duly reported to the head of police, who, laughingly and with much shaking of the head, turned my 'serious reprimand' into a most cordial interview.

As a rider to the story of my first arrival, I would relate a story given by my namesake and Chief Officer. He had been sitting at the end of the salon table during the first visit of the Customs' officers, while they were diligently perusing the ship's papers and questioning me closely (if only they had known what they were really sitting on!). Suddenly, one of the men turned to him and asked to be shown to the toilet. That was something of a jolt to my Chief Officer, who had spent the previous two hours cramming the two toilets with cases from top to bottom, so that it was only just possible to bolt the doors afterwards and show them to be 'occupied'! He rose and beckoned the Customs official to follow as he led him a leisurely and circuitous route round the ship, all the time racking his brain for a way out of his dilemma. The first toilet showed 'red', and likewise the second, and so to the first again. At last, out of genuine compulsion, he sprang to the companionway with the words: 'Well, I don't know about you, but I personally can't wait any longer!' Once on deck he proceeded to urinate over the side. He turned to find the Customs official doing likewise over the other rail. As you know, when one cow in the stall begins to make water, the rest follow suit . . . .

And while on the subject of the merits (or demerits) of the convivial glass, I can never forget the doctor's advice to my good and trusted friend Consul Erling Naess:

'Consul Naess, you have reached the mature age of fifty — so, from now on, with the object in mind of achieving your second half-century, it is not only your privilege but your serious duty: have a glass of cognac or Dutch gin — but every day.'

14

Phoenician Adventure

Before I draw these memoirs to a close, I have a last little narration to recall.

From Preparatory School onwards I was always a Dennis the Menace, sorely troubling the female teachers as well as the male ones, to say nothing of my parents, brother and sister, and this continued with some variation in degree until I retired in Arendal at the age of sixty-seven.

I was now bored, and felt like a racing engine shaking itself to pieces because it is no longer connected up with the work for which it was built. Audacity and romance passed for ever — like a comet in its eccentric orbit.

With time on my hands, I turned my restless mind to continuing my studies of the famous Phoenician seafarers, explorers and merchants. Pondering the location of ancient Thule, my mind wandered from Tile to Tule to Tyle to Thule to Tylemorck to Tilemorck, at which point it dawned on me that it was the present-day district of Telemark. A logical extension of the Phoenician trading route to Cornwall in England would have been to follow the coast up to Scotland and make an easy crossing to south-east Norway, facilitated by the prevailing Westerly winds. They probably stumbled on the excellent harbour at the present-day port of Langesund, where they could proceed far inland with their ships. The adjacent territory would have provided all they required, including an abundance of timber ideal for ship-building. In the great forests was a profusion of game and fowl, while the rivers, lakes and estuaries teemed with fish. Small wonder that they settled there. I have elaborated on this theory in my book *Wooden Walls to Distant Shores*, where I also mention a Greek explorer and merchant, a certain Pytheas, born in Marseilles. He undertook a trading voyage to Thule about 330 BC, or some six hundred years after the Phoenicians had established a colony there.

In my research I read about an ancient cave named after St Michael. The entrance was located in a steep crag, rendering access very difficult. After a number of visits to the site I came to the conclusion that it had been an old cult-place, used by the Phoenicians, and that there could have been an entrance from the top of the crag. I found a suggestive heap of stones there, and my excitement grew.

Firstly, I searched out the owner of the land where the cave was located, and came to an agreement with him that he should open up the heap of stones, the bottom of which could conceal a hidden entrance to the cave. But after some time he informed me that he had found nothing but solid rock.

Stubborn as I am, I sought and got his permission to remove the obstacle with the help of dynamite. This involved bringing in a sporting young friend of mine who had had some military training in the use of explosives and who, moreover, knew how to get hold of some dynamite albeit illegally. Of course, the whole affair was illegal from start to finish, and we had no authority from the Antiquarian of the Realm to use explosives on any ancient monument. Our several trips to the area were both pleasant and exciting, and the blasting nothing short of madness. We had dynamite in plenty, and excessive charges resulted in showers of stones landing hundreds of metres away. Luckily no one got killed, but the owner did come running up on one occasion when a 300 kilo stone, after a flight of about 500 metres, landed in his back yard some fifty metres from his house. He was a nice, timid man, and, thank the Lord, not married. One of the blasts moved a boulder of about thirty tons some six or seven metres — but the result exceeded my most sanguine expectations: we had found *another* entrance to the cave!

We were just in the nick of time. That same afternoon I had a telephone call from the Antiquarian of the Realm in Oslo, courteously demanding to know what the hell was going on. The Carnival was over and Ash Wednesday was upon us — the Panamanian 'Burial of the Fish'. Revelry forgotten, I prepared to receive the sign of penance: a fine.

The Antiquarian reported me to the police, who eventually presented his claim for damages — a grand total equivalent to

£15,800 sterling. The fine was an additional £500. He was bent on making it hot for me. Priming myself with cognac, I decided to refuse to pay anything but the fine. Both of us now had our hackles up. The Antiquarian revised his claim and reduced it to £11,500.

'Out of the question,' I told him, and off we went to court. The judgement was all in my favour. The judge turned down both the claim for damages and the fine, and sentenced the Antiquarian to pay the costs.

I thought that I had won, but not a bit of it. He took the case to the Supreme court, which eventually wanted me to pay £1,000 for damages and a £400 fine. I refused again, but offered to pay the £400 and £100 in damages. This was finally accepted, almost four years after my initial offer to pay up the original £500. And think of the costs he had to pay for his litigiousness!

Poor old Madsen! But let me now administer extreme unction.

Of course, the newspapers had a whale of a time with it, blackening my character with a wealth of lurid prose — specially the scandal-mongering little paper the *Agderposten* — and showing numerous photos of the artefacts I had found and dutifully sent off to the Antiquarian of the Realm.

His appraisal betrays his utter ignorance.

The coins were inspected by a numismatics expert in the Myntkabinett (Cabinet of Coins) in Oslo, and found to date from Phoenicia, Carthage (circa 300 BC), Egypt (circa 300 BC) and Rome (14-41 AD, 98-117 AD and approximately 140 AD). Some other pieces described by the Antiquarian as 'weights' were actually coins too badly damaged to be identified.

I also caught him out over some pieces of a necklace. These had been collected in an eastern Mediterranean country and identified by a French ethnographer as parts of an ancient mosaic, dating from several hundred years BC. In fact, they came from a necklace I bought at Frankfurt airport, whose string I later broke, and the rest from a parted necklace of unpolished amber which I had bought in Copenhagen. The amber had recently been picked up from the beach there.

And finally, there were the oil lamps. During a tour in Tunis in 1948, I visited ancient Carthage to see the ruins of the Amphitheatre. Here I met an old Arab who offered to sell me the coins and three oil lamps which he had found in the ruins.

After the usual haggling, I bought the things he offered, unaware that they would one day end up in the headquarters of our Antiquarian of the Realm. Two of the lamps were damaged, but the third was in excellent order, and I kept that for myself. Our Antiquarian declared that the lamps originated in Iceland in the sixteenth century. That is plainly the opinion of an ignoramus who has never visited the catacombs outside Rome, where such lamps may be seen in their hundreds.

My stratagem in giving up part of my alleged finds is, of course, obvious. My experiment was fraught with peril in more ways than one, or, as the seamen have it, the worst dangers are not at sea.

So now, my dear Antiquarians, I have solved both the riddle of the artefacts and the cave, or at least that of the ancient secret entrance. And if that is not to your satisfaction (I shall probably never hear your ovation), I am nevertheless at peace with myself.

One more story about this Mr Madsen, who should be honoured with the title of 'Anecdote-monger of the Realm'. On Sunday 4th October 1987 Norwegian radio had broadcast an interview with him. And it would be an unforgivable sin if he did not visit every Senior Citizens' Home in the kingdom to relate this incredible but allegedly true story. Norwegian radio is nothing very special, but on this occasion Mr Madsen's contribution undoubtedly enriched the listeners, and particularly the stalwarts of the Senior Citizens' Homes. And what did his story amount to? A great long yarn about nothing. Or rather, about an old motor cycle, would you believe it, *the only one in the world* which had carried the 'I' flag from the International Code of Flags! I should like to know whether this flag was hoisted and lowered in the statutory manner, or whether it was intended to indicate infamy. And in the middle of this spirited discourse, he also lectured on the pros and cons of using a capital letter for the noun 'Antiquarian'. A live audience, while stifling a yawn, would undoubtedly have given shouts of applause for the old motor bike. And of course it only added to the delights of the occasion that this was all recounted in the (in)famous sing-song Bergen dialect. I wonder if I was born an *enfant terrible*, or only became one? Or is it that I was born under Scorpio?

I longed to get away from it all, to unchain myself from my

loneliness and get back to a living life, to my old self, to my natural environment, to turn the clock back — to 'get away from the goblin'. I decided to share my daughter's lodging in London. But with all my things packed and Pickford's van waiting at the door, I discovered a grinning hobgoblin crowning the load. I take him with me, wherever I go, it seems.

I shall at least see a lot more of my youngest daughter in London. We get on well, much like my father and myself, though I am the wrong side of seventy and she the right side of twenty. She wants to be a lawyer when she finishes her studies in England.

I am no longer active, and fear that my time of deeds — or follies — is running out. Would I, really, choose an uneventful life, one of bitter-sweet happiness rather than the one I have survived to see? The answer, after further contemplation of my tumbler, could be distilled into a telegram before which all such previous messages would fade into insignificance. But we must be satisfied with a quotation from Bernard Shaw's *Pygmalion*, Eliza Doolittle's: *Not bloody likely!*

Tangled was the vale of my youth — and so was the sequence. It was a merry life while it lasted. Am I addicted to satire, now towards the last when these lines make me lapse into a smile?

EPILOGUE

I had three children by my Norwegian wife, none with my German wife, and one, a girl, with my Chinese wife. I spent in all thirty-three years of dreary married life, intermingled with a number of happy amours with young girl friends. There will never be a number four wife, but, hopefully, many sweethearts are still in the offing.

Why can't a wife be a honey rather than a hussy? adoring rather than boring? Why is it so lovely when a little butterfly sweeps through your rooms, accompanies you on an outing, and then eagerly jumps into your bed, while married life destroys all your illusions? Why — as Professor Henry Higgins in *My Fair Lady* asks us — why cannot a girl be more like a man . . . ? Are we both hypocrites?

A well-preserved sixty-year old with a third young Chinese wife on his lap, and a strong, happy disengaged freeman ten years later: so was Captain Wilson at seventy — and so to the bitter end — *Faervik for Orders*: Let Go!*

At sundown, this would be my testament to masculinity, for one who has no love to give, such as I had once, and gave in its entirety to an unobtainable girl, an idol, Ada. Call it what you will, the all-consuming emotion, at once burning and freezing, elevating and flooring, solid as granite and nebulous as the stars, immovable as the pyramids yet giddy as a gipsy dance, has followed me, nay haunted me, down all the years. Seconds together were bought with eternities; living or dying mattered not so long as we were together. But it was not to be. I was left with empty hands, grasping at the desert wind . . . .

Das gibt nur einmal — kommt nimmer wieder — Das Kann das Leben, nur einmal geben.†

After that, all was fiction; anti-climax. How could it be otherwise, with a heart or brain merely organized for function? Are we not as we were then, just faces in the crowd?

---

* At our family burial place at Faervik, Tromøy Island, outside Arendal, I have placed an anchor. On the crown is a bronze plaque inscribed with the words *Faervik for Orders*. On each of the two flukes is another plaque, and one of these has now been inscribed 'Sea Captain Sigfried Wilson, 1919-1983'.

† 'It comes but once and never again, for life can only give it once' — free translation from the German.